D0065253

FROM PEANUTS
TO THE PRESSBOX

BY ELI GOLD

WITH M. B. ROBERTS

THOMAS NELSON
Since 1798

NASHVILLE DALLAS MEXICO CITY RIO DE JANEIRO BEIJING

© 2009 by Eli Gold and M.B. Roberts

All rights reserved. No portion of this book may be reproduced, stored in a retrieval system, or transmitted in any form or by any means—electronic, mechanical, photocopy, recording, scanning, or other—except for brief quotations in critical reviews or articles, without the prior written permission of the publisher.

Published in Nashville, Tennessee, by Thomas Nelson. Thomas Nelson is a registered trademark of Thomas Nelson, Inc.

Page design: Walter Petrie

Thomas Nelson, Inc., titles may be purchased in bulk for educational, business, fundraising, or sales promotional use. For information, please e-mail SpecialMarkets@ThomasNelson.com.

Library of Congress Control Number: 2009932868

ISBN: 978-1-4016-0436-3

Printed in the United States of America

09 10 11 12 13 QW 6 5 4 3 2 1

TO THE MEMORY OF MY UNDERSTANDING MOTHER, KEILY, WHO NEVER YELLED WHEN SHE ASKED HER SIXTEEN-YEAR-OLD SON, "ELI, WHERE ARE YOU?"—ONLY TO BE TOLD THAT I WAS IN SOME FARAWAY CITY, WATCHING A GAME.

AND TO MY WIFE, CLAUDETTE, WHO, WHILE I WAS OFF CHASING MY DREAM, KEPT THIS FAMILY GOING AND RAISED OUR WONDERFUL DAUGHTER, ELISE, INTO THE BEAUTIFUL WOMAN SHE IS TODAY.

Contents

Acknowledgments

HEY, GETCHA PEANUTS . . . GETCHA MADISON SQUARE GARDEN peanuts . . . Peanuts . . . Getcha Garden peanuts here!!! . . . I was on my way. I was in the door, and they were paying me to be there. I was a vendor for the Harry M. Stevens Company, selling peanuts inside the world's most famous arena . . . the Magic World of Madison Square Garden. Oh, how I loved that building. It was *the* place to be. It was where *I had* to work. I wasn't content necessarily selling peanuts for the rest of my just-beginning adult life, but it was the sports capital of the world. It was "The Garden." 'Nuff said. Now the hard part. How would a fuzzy-cheeked young teen selling peanuts turn that humble start into a career that provided entrée into the press boxes of that famed building and other great stadiums and arenas around the world? This is my story. A story complete with determination, hard work, lucky breaks, and a list of dear friends, supporters, and family members who helped open the doors to give me every opportunity to succeed.

As in my first two books, *Crimson Nation* and *Bear's Boys*, I have again been blessed with the opportunity to work with a woman who must be a glutton for punishment. She is the lady who took my hours and hours and hours of dictation and molded those wildly disparate thoughts into the book you hold in your hands today—"Casper the Friendly Ghost Writer," M. B. Roberts. She, along with her hugely talented husband and *Sports Illustrated* photographer Ron Modra, offered guidance, support, and "print-world know-how" to help this "electronic media guy" download his brain and get his thoughts from mouth to paper.

Others you'll read about, like Butch Owens and Martha Oliver, were always there, constantly with me behind the scenes. Can I describe all they've done for me? That will become evident as you turn the pages. But suffice it to say, they've had a front-row seat to this journey, and *never* would it have gotten this far without their unending and unconditional support and encouragement.

On the business side of things, a big thank-you is due to Larry Black, the producer of the DVD series *Stock Car Legends Reunion*, for giving me permission to use quotes from this project. The DVD is a treasure for NASCAR fans and is still available at www.sportsreunion. net or by calling (800) 820-5405. I must also thank my dear friend, Verne Lundquist of CBS Sports, for writing the foreword to this book. Knowing him and learning from him have made me a far better broadcaster, and he is truly a Hall of Famer both in the booth and as a friend.

In writing this book, I found that some of the facts from years and years ago were getting a little fuzzy. Thankfully, friends from my days in Brooklyn were able to jog my memory and fill in the occasional gaps. Dear friends from my Crimson Tide and NASCAR families were most helpful in: (1) augmenting my recollections and (2) reminding me of stories that just "had to be in the book," stories that usually had me as the punch line of a bad day at the office. "Remember to tell the story about the day you fell off the chair in Cincinnati." "Don't forget the Lubomir Yourin story." "Y'gotta tell about the day that Dale Earnhardt died." Well, all of those stories and many others are in the pages to come. Stories that will make you laugh; stories that will make you cry. But most important, they are all stories that helped pave my way *from peanuts to the press box.*

Foreword

IN LATE DECEMBER 1975, THE DALLAS COWBOYS VISITED THE
Minnesota Vikings in an NFL wild-card playoff game. These were the
Cowboys of Roger Staubach and Bob Lilly, Mel Renfro and Cliff
Harris, and Charlie Waters and Drew Pearson. These were the guys
who formed the core of the football squad that was first given the
nickname of "America's Team." The game they played that frigid
late afternoon in the old Metropolitan Stadium helped cement that
moniker. It was the game in which, on a fourth down at midfield very
late in the contest, Drew Pearson went deep down the right side of
the field, then cut toward the center at the 10-yard line. He caught
Roger Staubach's desperation pass, juggled it for a moment, then
cradled it as he crossed the goal line to give Dallas a 17-14 lead. They
won the game, and the play became famous as the Staubach-to-
Pearson "Hail Mary pass."

I was the Cowboys' radio play-by-play man during the 1970s. For
that one game, the late Frank Glieber, a dear friend and a mentor
who had a long and distinguished career at CBS Sports, was available

to work the game with me. We flipped a coin to decide who would do which half as the lead broadcaster. Frank won the toss and said, "I'll do the second half."

That meant I would do play-by-play for the first half, "color" for the second, and then head down to the field with five minutes remaining in the game to get ready for the postgame locker-room show.

And so, with less than a minute to play, I found myself on the Cowboys' sideline, near the 50-yard line, when Drew Pearson caught the winning pass. The Minnesota crowd grew surly as Dallas lined up to kick off.

They were convinced beyond doubt that Pearson had shoved off of defender Nate Wright and had committed offensive pass interference in order to make himself available for the reception. (In a quiet moment, Drew will admit that he probably did.)

Just before the subsequent kickoff, a drunken fool in the south end zone stands heaved an empty whiskey bottle toward the field. With a sickening thud, it hit back judge Armen Terzian in the head and knocked him unconscious. It was a terribly frightening moment, and though the crowd became quiet for a moment as medical officials took care of Terzian's needs, they returned to their raucous behavior once he was taken from the field.

As the game ended, I was standing by the side of Rayfield Wright, the Cowboys' wonderfully gifted offensive tackle who was selected to the Pro Football Hall of Fame in 2006. While Rayfield was six foot seven, 285 pounds, and nicknamed Big Cat, I've never seen the north side of five foot nine. He had his helmet on his head and a huge blue cape around his shoulders. As he sensed the increasing possibility of unruly crowd behavior as we left the field, he looked down at me and said, "Little buddy, this could get nasty. I want you to walk to the tunnel with Big Cat." That's the way we exited the field in the aftermath of the Cowboys' Hail Mary victory, Big Cat and Little Buddy, Rayfield

Wright holding his huge, blue cape over his little buddy's head in case anyone couldn't resist the temptation to hurl objects in our direction.

I shared this story with my dear friend, Eli Gold, a couple of years ago. I did so because I wanted him to know that though I'm very appreciative of the splendid opportunities I've been given to work in a variety of venues in a quarter of a century at CBS Sports, I still miss the special relationship a sports broadcaster has with his audience and with his community if he spends most of his time with one team or with one university.

In my case, it was sixteen years with the Dallas Cowboys, a group of players and fans for whom I still feel a special bond. In Eli's case, it's his ongoing commitment to the Crimson Tide of the University of Alabama.

This is Eli's story. It's the story of a young boy growing up in Brooklyn who had a dream of someday earning the privilege of sitting in the "best seat in the house" and serving as the eyes, the ears, and, most significant, the voice through which listeners and fans learned the fate of the team they loved. It is the story of how the kid from Brooklyn's dream was fulfilled in the unlikely environs of the city of Tuscaloosa and the state of Alabama and the entire region of the southeastern United States. There are a few highs, a few lows, and a few curveballs in the tale.

How successful has he become? Let me share a story from the 2008 Alabama–Auburn game in Tuscaloosa.

Our CBS production crew was having dinner in a terrific downtown restaurant on the Friday night before the game. A fan approached our table of six and tapped me on the shoulder. As I turned in his direction, he said, "Eli, I really, really enjoy your broadcasts."

Rather than embarrass him by correcting him and telling him he had the wrong guy, I simply murmured thanks and turned back to our group.

An hour later, as we were paying our bill, the manager asked if he could take a picture with Gary Danielson, our analyst; Tracy Wolfson, our sideline reporter; and me. Sure, we said, and got into position. As soon as the picture had been snapped, the same fellow who had tapped me on the shoulder earlier tapped me on the shoulder again and said, "Eli, could I take a picture with you?"

"I'll be glad to take a picture with you," I said, "but you should know that I'm not Eli Gold."

"Well, who are you then?" he inquired.

"Last name is Lundquist," I answered.

"Well, you ought to be Eli Gold."

That's the kind of loyalty my friend inspires. Enjoy his story.

— Verne Lundquist

CBS Sports

ONE

The Kid on the D-Train

YEARS AGO, I WAS FLYING BACK TO BIRMINGHAM AFTER DOING my *NASCAR Live* radio show in Daytona Beach, Florida. I'd made this flight hundreds of times, so I had become very friendly with the Delta gate agents in both the Atlanta and Daytona airports.

I was standing near the gate, waiting to be confirmed for a frequent-flier upgrade, when I noticed another gentleman standing nearby. It was Neil Armstrong, the astronaut.

I recognized Armstrong, who also happened to be waiting for an upgrade, and my friend, the gate agent, introduced us. I was glad to shake hands with this great American hero who became the first man to walk on the moon during the 1969 *Apollo 11* mission.

Soon the upgrades became available, and my friend was preparing our boarding passes. Evidently there were just two seats left, an aisle and a window seat. The gate agent leaned over to me and whispered, "Which one do you want?"

Armstrong overheard him and asked, "How come you asked him which seat he wanted? Why didn't you ask me?"

"Mr. Armstrong," my friend replied, "by now, a whole bunch of folks have walked on the moon. But there's only one Voice of the Crimson Tide."

We all had a belly laugh about that one! But I have to say, it's true that Alabama fans are everywhere! And often the ones who stay closest to home are the most dedicated, passionate, zealous, deeply loyal people I could have ever imagined in my wildest dreams. It has been my great pleasure and privilege to be the Voice of the Crimson Tide for more than twenty years. Without a doubt, this is the best job in the broadcast business, and I wouldn't give it up for a round-trip ticket to the moon.

As a little boy growing up in Brooklyn in the '60s, and later, as a teenager who got a job selling peanuts at Madison Square Garden, I dreamed about having a job exactly like this one. When I think back, the picture in my mind is in black and white. But it's not at all fuzzy. I loved talking about sports. And I knew what I wanted to do.

Brooklyn, New York, circa 1968, my childhood home—the lower floor of a duplex right off Flatbush Avenue—was just a few short blocks from Midwood High School. I could cover the distance in about ten minutes if I didn't dally. The thing was, though, I usually didn't make it there. Most mornings, I got up, got dressed, and ate breakfast like every other kid on my street. Then I'd walk with my friends to school, but that's as far as I went. I'd watch them turn into the school yard, then I'd keep on walking, toward the Avenue J subway station. I'd climb up the stairs to the subway platform, pay my fare, and board the D-train to Manhattan. No offense to Mrs. Picheny, but I had no interest in sitting in her class, learning to do logarithms. My vast fifteen years of life experience told me that a working knowledge of logarithms wouldn't help me become what I wanted to be—a sports broadcaster. So I'd take the train into the city or into the Bronx to watch Yankees games. (I told my parents I was researching my future vocation.) Or I went to my part-time job selling peanuts at Madison Square Garden so I could watch basketball and hockey games (more research). Or, as I became more enterprising, I would go to one of my many internships and part-time jobs in and around the world of sports broadcasting. Maybe it sounds like a ready-made excuse for a kid who didn't like to sit in class, but somehow I knew I wasn't going to learn about my chosen trade in a book. I knew I had a lot to learn; therefore I skipped school and went searching for what I needed to know.

I was a huge sports fan as a kid. In my neighborhood how could you not be? New York had so many legendary teams in the 1950s and '60s. When it came to baseball, I was a Yankees fan. I'd like to say I was discerning in my choice of teams to follow, but truth be told, I pulled for the Bronx Bombers because from 1957 (when the Dodgers and Giants left for California) to 1962 (when the Mets began play), the Yankees were literally the only baseball team in town.

I remember vividly my first trip to Yankee Stadium in the Bronx. I was about four years old, and my dad took me to a game between the Yankees and the Cleveland Indians on a Wednesday afternoon. The funny thing was, my dad wasn't a big sports fan. If it was up to him, he wouldn't be at a Yankees game on a Wednesday afternoon or even on a Saturday, but he knew I wanted to go. So we went. I don't know how he got the seats that day, but we sat in the second row, right behind the Indians' dugout. Rocky Colavito hit a two-run homer for the Cleveland Indians, but the Yankees crushed them, 10-2.

When I was a little older, I took my mom to a Yankees game. Like my father, she wasn't a huge sports fan—she'd rather go to a Broadway show—but one Mother's Day I got her two tickets to a Yankees game.

Being the selfless son that I was, I offered to use the other ticket and take her to the game. Turns out there were quite a few moms at the game that day. The Yankees even gave away packages of Hostess Twinkies with special Happy Mother's Day stickers on them. As always, it was a great game.

I didn't really have a favorite player, but I did like Elston Howard, the catcher. I thought he was so cool with that big number 32 on his back. I was more a fan of the team than of any one guy. I didn't care if Bill "Moose" Skowron was playing first base or if Bobby Richardson was at second. It didn't matter to me if the winning run was hit by Mickey Mantle, Roger Maris, or Hector Lopez! Just as long as the Yanks came out on top.

Still, even though I was mostly a "team guy" and all of eight years old, I followed the Mantle-Maris home-run race of 1961, just like everyone else. Mickey Mantle was already a huge Yankees star, and Roger Maris, who was traded from the Kansas City Athletics in 1960, was rising fast. A few weeks into the '61 season, it was clear these two teammates were both on pace to tie or beat Babe Ruth's single-season record of 60 home runs. First Mantle pulled ahead. Who didn't want to cheer for a guy whom manager Casey Stengel described as a better player on one leg than anybody else was on two? Then, at the end of July, Maris took the lead with 40 home runs to Mantle's 39. Exciting stuff. By the first of September, the count was Maris 51, Mantle 48, but unfortunately, nagging injuries and an infection sidelined Mantle for a series of games and the MVP of '56, '57, and later, '62, was out of the hunt.

Despite intense pressure from Mantle's fans and those not wanting to see Ruth's record shattered by any player, Maris persevered. He kept up his incredible performance at the plate despite constant talk of "the asterisk," which refers to the mark the commissioner of baseball said would be affixed to Maris's name in the book if he broke the record in the last eight games of the season (because the '61 Yankees played eight more games than in Ruth's day).

I don't remember paying much attention to the asterisk discussions or participating in any Maris bashing. For one thing, I thought and still think records are made to be broken. I really just wanted the Yankees to win. And that year they won big. Maris, Mantle, Yogi Berra, Whitey Ford, Johnny Blanchard, and company beat the Reds in the World Series, and all was right with my world.

Like most kids back then, I had a little black transistor radio with one of those plug-in earpiece attachments. I used to carry it with me everywhere. (Note to people under age thirty: it was like an iPod, only much bigger and heavier, and you had to listen to what the DJ played on the radio instead of punching up your choice of five thousand songs.) I listened to ball games constantly. I couldn't begin to calculate the hours I spent listening to Mel Allen and Red Barber announcing the Yankees games. Interestingly, especially in light of my future Alabama connection, both gentlemen hailed from the South. Allen, whose real name was Melvin Avrom Israel, was born in Birmingham, Alabama. Barber's hometown was Columbus, Mississippi.

Both broadcasters projected a Southern friendliness that was quite a contrast to the typical New York approach, and New Yorkers embraced them. Both were incredibly beloved in New York. Neither man could go anywhere in the five boroughs without being stopped by a fan, especially after a Yankees win.

Barber's days in the Yankees booth were preceded by fourteen years as the Voice of the Dodgers (and four years with the Cincinnati Reds before that). According to Bob Costas, the erudite Barber combined a tremendous reporting skill with a lyric patter. The guy was so at ease, it's said he sat back from the microphone and chatted with his listeners, never failing to pepper his commentary with mentions of rhubarb or a player being in "the catbird seat."

Talk-show host and New York native Larry King once told Costas that you could walk down any street in Brooklyn during Barber's era and not miss a pitch because somebody would have a window open and his game-day voice would loft out. If a cab stopped, you'd hear Barber calling the game from Ebbets Field, although his voice might be obscured by the cabbie complaining that "the guy is too fair." Barber always called it straight.

Mel Allen called it straight, too, but when it came to enthusiasm, he had the edge. If I had to pick a favorite broadcaster from that era, it would be Allen. He was such an easy listen and so versatile. He was best known as the "Legendary Voice of the Yankees," but he also did the Giants and Redskins, as well as broadcasts for the World Series, all-star games, Rose Bowls and Orange Bowls, and later, the TV show *This Week in Baseball*. And I shouldn't fail to mention that he got his start as the Voice of the Crimson Tide. So when I say our paths eventually crossed, I mean that literally.

Not only was he great to listen to (I once heard someone say, "Allen let the game breathe."), but he also had a great life story. Growing up in Alabama, Allen learned to read at a very young age, courtesy of the Sears & Roebuck catalog, which he would peruse while occupying the family's outhouse. Then he would come inside, point at pictures of baseball bats and gloves, and ask his parents to read him the text next to the pictures, which he would repeat until he'd learned the words.

Allen skipped several grades in school (unlike myself, who simply skipped *school*), then went on to the University of Alabama, eventually earning a law degree. But a career in law was not meant to be. Allen's love of baseball led him to become a sports columnist, then a radio announcer. While a student at the university, Allen became the PA announcer for Alabama football games. Then, in 1933, legendary coach Frank Thomas recommended him for the job as Alabama's play-by-play man, and he called the Tide's games for four seasons.

In 1937 he took a vacation to New York City, and after auditioning for and landing a job as a CBS Radio Network staff announcer, he ended up staying there (between his travels as a broadcaster) for the rest of his life. Allen, who took his father's middle name as his new, on-air last name, was paid forty-five dollars a week to do newscasts, sometimes giving on-air descriptions of big events, such as the crash of the *Hindenburg*. Catastrophes were not how he would make his name, though, unless you count the time he lost his voice during the 1963 World Series, in which the Dodgers defeated the Yankees in a four-game sweep.

Allen wanted to do baseball and got his first assignment working as a color analyst (the guy who sits next to the play-by-play announcer and fills in stats and commentary between plays) for the 1938 World Series after his bosses heard him broadcast a long, ad-libbed description of the Vanderbilt Cup race, which he did from an airplane flying overhead.

His big break came in 1939, when he was tapped to replace Yankees assistant broadcaster Garnett Marks, who twice mispronounced the name of Ivory Soap, a major sponsor, by saying, "Ladies, gather 'round your sets, because I want to talk to you about Ovary Soap . . ."

Each time he made the gaffe, Marks tried to correct himself but couldn't quit laughing. Allen soon replaced him.

Over time, Allen became synonymous with the Yankees to so many fans. And one of them was me.

On the rare occasions I actually went to school, I'd bring my radio along, especially during the World Series, which in those days was a daytime event. I also tuned in if there was a big news event pending; I was, and still am, a big news junkie. So when John Glenn became the first American to orbit the earth in February 1962, I listened to reports off and on all day long. I'd sneak the radio into the bathroom or the hallway to listen. Or, when I was sitting at my desk, I'd run the wire up my sleeve and stick that little earpiece in my ear and get a quick update when the teacher wasn't looking.

When it came to games, as frequently as possible I'd check the scores and give updates to my friends. I would cough every time one of the teams scored. If they scored two runs I'd cough twice. God forbid they had a big inning. I'd be on my way to see the school nurse!

At nighttime I used to take the radio to bed with me and sit underneath my blankets and listen to games when I was supposed to be asleep. I'd listen to hockey or occasionally basketball, but most often I remember tuning in baseball games. In New York in the '60s, you could pick up seven or eight different MLB broadcasts on any given night from April to September. I always tried to catch the last few innings of a game, especially if the Yankees were playing. I'd turn up Allen and Barber as loud as I dared; then, if my parents came in and said, "Time to go to sleep!" I'd ditch the radio until they were gone. Then I'd turn the sound back up just as Allen exclaimed, "How 'bout that!" and close my eyes as I conjured up the scene at the ballpark. I'd adjust the volume down low so only I could hear it, then I'd lie on my right side and put the radio speaker directly under my right ear. I went to sleep that way— listening to an eighth-inning lullaby—too many nights to count. I almost always nodded off before the end of the game, and I never seemed to wake up to click the radio off; therefore in the morning my first order of business was to grab a paper and find out the final score. And get some new batteries.

Baseball was big, but I loved football too. In New York most football fans followed the Giants, the old-guard team that had been around for years. I really wanted to go to some games, but the Giants season ticket list probably held some fifty thousand names. People left tickets in their wills. But the average person was never going to get them. You could buy tickets to the New York Titans, though, the new American Football League (AFL) team that would later become the New York Jets.

My dad and I got Titans season tickets and went to the games at the New York Polo Grounds, which resembled an open-air mausoleum. Even though it was chock-full of history, (the New York Giants' football team played there until 1955), in its latter years, the Polo Grounds was like the world's largest outdoor toilet. It had really gone downhill.

According to Giants broadcaster Marty Glickman, the working conditions were less than glamorous at the Polo Grounds even prior to the Titans years. Evidently he would call the games from inside the scoreboard in right field. The broadcast crew would peer through the slats to see, and the work space was so narrow that the first one in was the last to leave.

As for us, in order to see the Titans play, we sat in this old, decrepit ballpark, surrounded by rats that were oftentimes bigger than the linemen on the field. The upside was, if you bought Titans season tickets at the Polo Grounds, you were guaranteed the opportunity to buy tickets at the new ballpark when the team moved to Shea Stadium in Queens. So, in 1964, when the Titans moved to William A. Shea Municipal Stadium and changed their name to the New York Jets (due to the venue's proximity to LaGuardia Airport), we followed them there.

Shea Stadium, which was torn down in 2008 to make room for additional parking for the new, adjacent Citi Field, was a marvel in its day. It had a bold orange and blue facade, brilliant green grass, vibrant yellow field boxes, tons of bright lights across its upper reaches, and big, wide concourses. Your ticket stub matched the color of one of the 57,343 new green, red, yellow, or blue seats. (Ours were in the upper deck, in the corner of the end zone.)

Broadcasters benefited from better working conditions at Shea, although they did have to contend with noise from the airport. At first, anyway. It wasn't long before air traffic control fell in line, and flight paths were diverted to prevent rumbling planes from drowning out game-day broadcasts on radio and TV.

The Jets shared the new stadium with the fledgling New York Metropolitans, known universally as the Mets, the National League expansion team brought to New York in 1962 (they also played initially at the Polo Grounds) after the exit of the Dodgers and baseball Giants in 1957. Even as a die-hard Yankees fan, I never hated the Mets. Along with everyone else, during their first few seasons I just laughed at them. New York fans called them "bums" (*They're bums, but they're our bums*), but most of the media called them the Lovable Losers. Even one of their own broadcasters, Lindsey Nelson, referred to the early Mets as "the biggest dog that ever was under."

The problem was that the Mets ownership attempted to attract former Dodgers and Giants fans by stacking their roster with old Dodgers and Giants players—guys who should have stayed retired. In another nod to nostalgia, the great Yankees manager Casey Stengel was coaxed from retirement to lead the Mets. But even Stengel couldn't save this bunch. Only the 1899 Cleveland Spiders lost more games in a season (134) than the 1962 Mets (120).

Of course, the Mets turned things around a few years later, winning the World Series in 1969. They went from the Lovable Losers to the Miracle Mets in just seven years! They've gone on to notch many more successful seasons, but in the beginning the home team's on-field play was awful, even though the field was picture-perfect.

One guy who never doubted the appeal of the new stadium was Jets owner Sonny Werblin. Before the first game was played at Shea, Werblin publicly boasted that his team would draw twenty-five thousand fans. Since the Titans/Jets had been drawing an average of five to six thousand fans at the old Polo Grounds, nobody believed him.

Then a funny thing happened. Maybe it was the allure of the World's Fair going on right next door. Or maybe it was the shiny new venue and its equally shiny new team. Whatever it was, people came in droves.

In broadcast historian Curt Smith's book *Of Mikes and Men*, Jets broadcaster Merle Harmon told a story about his partner, Otto Graham, driving from his house in Connecticut to the team's very first home game. According to Harmon, at 7:45 p.m. there were already twenty-five thousand fans gathered for an 8:00 p.m. start. The problem was, Graham hadn't arrived. So Harmon did the pregame show without him. Then, the powers-that-be delayed the game so the crowd could make their way in. By kickoff, there were some forty-three thousand people in their seats. But no Graham. So Harmon did the entire first half alone. At halftime, Graham showed up. "Where have you been?" Harmon asked.

Graham's answer? "Listening to you. I've been sitting out there on the Grand Central Parkway for the whole first half."

After that, people believed Sonny Werblin. It's hard to remember how different things were back then, but when the Jets first came to New York, they were interlopers, the new guys in town. Some fans, myself included, initially got more excited about the visiting teams than the hometown guys. It was really cool to be at Shea the first time established NFL teams like the Green Bay Packers or the Chicago Bears came to play. That made up for the year or two I sat in the stands watching the New York Titans play the AFL's Boston Patriots, as they were called back then, or the Buffalo Bills. I mean, who the heck were the Buffalo Bills? Granted, they had some great players, like Daryle Lamonica. And another charter AFL team, the Kansas City Chiefs, had one of the greatest quarterbacks in the history of the game in Len Dawson. But who were these guys?

It wasn't long before the upstart AFL teams began to command respect. I remember when the Denver Broncos came in to play. They had a coach that was so good you knew the Jets were probably going to lose. The Oakland Raiders had a big rivalry with the Jets, and when they came into town, you knew the Jets were in for it because the Raiders had one of the best quarterbacks anyone had ever seen. New York fans booed the Broncos' coach and the Raiders' quarterback, but we secretly wished these guys could be on our side, because they always won. The only way we could give them a pseudotribute was to boo the stuffing out of them!

I told this story recently at a University of Alabama football banquet because it has a strong Alabama connection. Coincidentally, the Broncos' coach I was referring to was Lou Saban, the cousin of Nick Saban, who was named head coach of the Crimson Tide in 2007. And the quarterback? None other than Kenny Stabler, the former Alabama star turned NFL MVP, who also was my longtime color man for Alabama football games.

When I told this story, Coach Saban gave a nod of recognition and managed a grin. (Maybe he knows when he gets booed at Alabama road games, it's a perverse tribute to being a winner.) And Stabler? He laughed out loud at remembering the Raiders' visits to Shea and said, "Well, we used to like to come in there and beat ya!"

From the start, the AFL teams were different. The referees wore red-and-white–striped shirts, as opposed to the traditional zebra black and white. Anything to add some color! The owners were a bunch of rich men who had the audacity to challenge the existing football league. Back in the 1960s, *expansion* was a foreign word. The National Hockey League was still in its original six-team format. Major League Baseball had not expanded yet; a few of its franchises had relocated, but the huge growth spurt was still years away. The same thing was true with basketball. The NBA had the Cincinnati Royals, the Boston Celtics, the Minneapolis Lakers, and the New York Knicks. Leagues were still in their original incarnations.

Then along come these guys who not only dared to challenge the status quo but were bold enough to be successful!

Probably the strongest sign that the AFL had arrived, from a broadcast point of view, anyway, was the famous "Heidi Game" in November 1968. The Jets were playing the Raiders, and as the game clock ran down, the Jets were ahead, apparently headed for victory. Network execs decided to cut away from the game and begin the regularly scheduled *Heidi* movie, which they expected to get huge ratings.

Much to everyone's surprise, the Raiders scored two touchdowns in the last few minutes and won the ball game. Fans on the East Coast missed the outcome and were furious (West Coast fans saw it live due to the time difference.) They flooded the network and league headquarters in New York with angry phone calls and letters.

Although the Heidi Game was bad news for the Jets' rivalry with the Raiders, it was good news for the league as a whole and made the networks stand up and take notice. As for the Jets, they were getting plenty of notice on and off the field. They were a flashy, ritzy group of players whose popularity skyrocketed as they began to morph into a winning franchise. When a young quarterback named Joe Willie Namath came to town in 1965 (fresh from the University of Alabama), things got seriously exciting. Namath's three-year, $427,000 contract made him the highest paid player in pro football history, and he soon became as well-known for his glamorous New York–bachelor lifestyle (think llama rugs, a big fur coat, and a girl on each arm) as he did for his powerful throwing arm. But behind all that style was plenty of substance.

In 1969 the Namath-led Jets had won their way into the third ever NFL-AFL Championship game, which was also referred to for the first time as the Super Bowl. (The first two championship games were retroactively called Super Bowls.) My dad and I couldn't afford to travel to the game, which was being played at the Orange Bowl in

Miami, so we did the next best thing. We went over to our neighbors' (the Speiglers') house, and watched the game there. Hi-def hadn't been invented, and there weren't any big-screen TVs in those days, but their screen was bigger than ours, so that's where we went.

The Jets, coached by Weeb Ewbank, were huge underdogs coming into the game against the more established and experienced Don Shula–led Baltimore Colts. Some writers had predicted the Colts to win by as much as twenty points. Then, before the game, Joe made his famous claim. "We'll win," he said. "I guarantee it."

The game was broadcast on NBC-TV, and knowing me, I was probably just as enthralled with the color commentary of Al DeRogatis and Kyle Rote, and with Curt Gowdy's play-by-play, as I was with the game.

Gowdy was so good. He called it straight. When describing his broadcast philosophy, he used to say, "Keep it simple, do your homework, give the score, and leave the cheering to the fans."

As a broadcaster, I agree with his philosophy. But that day I was a fan, and I cheered—no, screamed—for the duration of the game. Namath completed 17 of 28 passes for 206 yards, then trotted off the field, holding up his index finger when the Jets won. I'll never forget that sight. It was absolutely magnificent.

As thrilling as it was to grow up watching Joe Namath throw the football and Mickey Mantle hit the baseball, hockey was my favorite sport. Later in our high school years, three buddies—Howard Steinhart, Joe Resnick, and Steve Sobo—and I splurged heavily on New York Rangers season tickets that ran us $2.50 a game for seats in section 440, row F. These were the blue seats at Madison Square Garden—behind the nets, way at the end of the rink. I still have the ticket stubs!

Steve passed away awhile ago, but I've kept in touch with both Howard, who is a schoolteacher in New York City, and Joe, a long-time Associated Press sports writer who lives in Los Angeles. For years I've picked up the newspaper and seen Joe's byline in the sports section. Or I've watch some coach give a press conference and seen Joe, front and center, in the gaggle of reporters!

We loved watching those games, despite having to squint to see Eddie Giacomin or Caesar Maniago making a big save, or Rod Gilbert scoring a big goal. I mean, we were up high. One more row up and we'd be on the roof. The only up-close player sightings we managed from that vantage point were of injured players. Sometimes when guys got hurt, they'd come up and watch the game from the press box, which wasn't far from our seats. They'd take the elevator up from the locker room and walk past us on their way to the press box. We'd yell out their names like idiots!

No matter where I was in relation to the game action, truth be told, I was always more interested in the broadcasters than the players. No matter what sport I was watching, I always spent most of my time turning my binoculars up to the press box to spot this broadcaster or that play-by-play guy. While my friends were watching the Yankees shift the outfield against a certain hitter, I was riveted on the guys behind the microphones. There I was, in the cheap seats, looking through my binoculars just to watch some guy talk! When we were at the Garden, I would make my way over to the broadcast booth between periods to see and hear what was going on. I wouldn't go in or talk to anybody. I just wanted to be near it. A little sick, I know! But watching the broadcasters and listening to them made it a little more real. Maybe one day, I thought, I'd be up there too.

TWO

Pittsburgh? What Are You Doing in Pittsburgh?

IT'S HARD TO PIN DOWN WHEN I FIRST FELL IN LOVE WITH TALKING about sports. I played Little League baseball and was a pretty good first baseman, but from as early as I can remember, I loved watching sporting events. I was a big sports fan. You might say I was a super-spectator. And somehow that translated into me wanting to be the one describing things.

When I was in the eighth grade, all the kids wrote their future occupation under their school pictures in the yearbook. My declaration? Sports broadcaster. The kids also voted on imaginary gifts they would leave to their classmates. My present? New York Rangers season tickets.

Although sports was my main area of interest, I was intrigued by anything that had to do with broadcasting or journalism. I was eaten up with it!

Like everybody in New York, I used to listen to WABC radio, the preeminent rock-and-roll station of its time. A lot of the really famous rock-and-roll DJs worked there, including Cousin Brucie, the guy who introduced the Beatles at their famous Shea Stadium concert in 1965, and Dan Ingram, arguably the best Top 40 DJ of all time. Then one day, when I was fourteen, the station announced a contest where a certain number of kids could win the chance to come up to the studio in Manhattan for a question-and-answer session with the DJs. All you had to do was write a one- or two-paragraph essay about why you should be selected as one of the lucky few to visit the studio. With high hopes I wrote a few sentences, something about how much I wanted to be a broadcaster, and sent it off. Then I waited.

Every day I'd run out to the mailbox and hope against all hope that I would get the letter from WABC. Weeks went by. Then one day there was a big snowstorm in Brooklyn. But as the saying goes, "Neither snow nor rain nor heat nor gloom of night stays these couriers from the swift completion of their appointed rounds." So when I saw the mailman walking down the street, I put on my galoshes and trudged through the snow to the street corner to get the mail. I couldn't believe it. There was the letter from WABC! I opened it right where I stood. Yes! I had been selected to attend the press conference!

I was so excited I started running back to the house, which was about thirty yards away. Well, the snow was up to about midcalf, and wouldn't you know, I tripped and fell. All I could think about as my glasses went flying off my head and I started tumbling to the ground was, *I can't let anything happen to this letter!* Somehow I managed to hold it high above my head! The next thing I know, I'm lying there like a beached whale in a giant snowdrift. But son of a gun, that letter stayed dry! I was completely focused on keeping that letter intact so I could present it to the people at the studio. I could not allow it to be damaged in any way. As if the snow might erase the words!

I had no interest in being a disc jockey at all, but I still wanted to be at that press conference, because that's what broadcasters did. They went to press conferences and interviewed people. Here I was, just a fourteen-year-old kid, and I'm meeting Dan Ingram and Cousin Brucie. It was spectacular!

I guess writing that letter to WABC and actually getting a response sparked something in my brain, because not long after that, I got out the old Royal manual typewriter we had at the house and started writing letters to every sportscaster I could think of—both New York–area broadcasters and national guys. I actually did this off and on for the next few years. I wrote to Bob Wolff, the Hall of Fame broadcaster, who at the time was the TV Voice of the New York Knicks and the New York Rangers. I wrote to Jim Gordon, the radio Voice of the Rangers. I wrote to Mel Allen and Red Barber, who did the Yankees games. I wrote to Chip Cipolla, the sports director at WNEW Radio, who also worked on the broadcast crew for the New York Giants. I wrote to Dan Kelly, the Voice of the St. Louis Blues, who was the preeminent broadcaster of hockey in the United States. And I wrote to Curt Gowdy, who basically defined network sports broadcasting. I asked all these guys the same questions: How did you start? What classes should I take in college? Any advice? Incredibly, almost everybody responded! Most of these sportscasters sent back short notes, some with pointed, practical suggestions.

For instance, Curt Gowdy advised taking as many English and journalism classes as possible and getting a job with a station of any size in any town that would allow me to get on-the-air experience. He emphasized that early in your career, no job is too small. Gowdy started out making eighteen dollars a week at a station in Wyoming, where every morning he did the farm report before he read the sports scores. He also had to sweep the floors! And he said he wouldn't trade that experience for anything.

Bob Wolff suggested I get a tape recorder and practice calling the play-by-play at high school games or at home in front of the TV, with the sound turned off. This was great advice, and I immediately sprang for a reel-to-reel tape machine that I kept in the house, and a cassette tape recorder, a huge thing the size of a small microwave oven that I brought with me to games.

Besides asking for career advice, I always made sure to ask these broadcasters (via letter, or in person if I got the opportunity), "Is there any way I could help you out? Could I come watch you work? Would you mind if I tagged along?" Kind of brash, I admit. But how else would I kick the door ajar and edge my way inside?

I soon started showing up at different radio stations just to watch and learn. People were really nice about it if I was quiet and didn't get in the way. Chip Cipolla at WNEW said, "Sure. C'mon up. You can hang around. We're not going to pay you anything, but you can hang around." So I did.

My dad knew some folks at WOR in New York, a great radio station, 710 on the AM dial. It was the leading adult radio station—heavy on news, light on music. Its claim to fame was *Rambling with Gambling*, the morning show that first began in 1925 with host John B. Gambling. The show was innovative in that it was all talk. By the '60s the show was being hosted by John A. Gambling, who had followed his father into the role. He did weather, consumer reports, sports, and the first-ever helicopter traffic reports. Gambling had Howard Stern–like ratings in his day, but the similarities with Stern end there. The show was very benign. Not racy at all. His son, John R. Gambling, took over for him in 1991, and in 2000 moved over to WABC after a seventy-five-year run at WOR.

So I'd go up to WOR and just hang around and watch people. Even on the weekends. I'd just sit there while they logged commercials. In the late '60s they didn't have automated logging systems, like they do today. Back then, every time a commercial was played, a guy in the studio would note it on the paper log. This was the affidavit that said, *Yes, indeed, the commercial ran,* so the station could bill the advertiser.

I spent many, many days just sitting there with the guy who was logging stuff. Then I'd go into the newsroom and watch the guys work. Some of them not only were nice to me but actually took the time to teach me a few things. They'd let me work on the equipment sometimes, just to practice. Or they'd hand me a piece of copy off the Associated Press (AP) machine, the old rip-and-read wire, and ask me if I wanted to rewrite it for them.

On-air announcers never read the copy exactly as it came off the wire. They always rewrote it, or someone they worked with rewrote it, to give it a different slant. Stations wanted to be sure to change the wording so that what was said on air was not the same thing being said on another station in Wichita, Kansas. It had to be different. So they let me rewrite copy. Basically, I was like a sponge. Listening, watching, and learning.

As I mentioned earlier, even though he sometimes took me to games, my dad wasn't a big sports fan. He wouldn't have known an inside-the-park home run from a ground-rule double, but he took me to Yankees games. He could have done without going to see the Titans or the Jets, but he went. He did it for me.

When I was fifteen, my dad died of stomach cancer. He had been sick for a year or two before he finally passed away, always in and out of the doctor's office or the hospital. I knew he was very, very ill, but I really didn't know the true extent of it. My mom tried to shield me from the details, and I simply couldn't imagine the possibility of him actually being gone.

For most of my father's working life, he was the executive director of the Brooklyn Jewish Center, which was a combination synagogue/ community center, a prominent place that was the hub of our community. One thing I remember about him is that he always treated everyone at work with respect, from the switchboard operators and maintenance guys to his fellow board members in the national organization.

A lot of very highly placed New Yorkers were members of the Brooklyn Jewish Center, for instance, the future mayor of New York, Abraham Beame. In that sense my father was very well connected. Maybe that's how we got those Yankees tickets right behind the dugout!

But what sticks out in my mind are not the privileges or special favors his position may have brought. Instead, I remember him treating people well. A handyman who worked at the center would come to our house to fix something, and although the guy said it was his pleasure to do it, my dad would be adamant about paying him. Or the caterer, Stanley Kotimsky, would offer to give my dad a leftover chicken after a big event, but Dad would insist on buying it from him. Or the superintendent, Andy Hoolihan, who headed up the maintenance division. He was a Catholic but would come to work on Jewish High Holy days, wearing a suit and tie out of respect for my dad and the other folks at the center.

It seemed like my father, this six-foot-tall, lean, hardworking man, had such a wonderful way with people. When there were problems, he always seemed to find a way to work them out. To this day, I try to remember his methods and his philosophy. Everybody counts. Everybody contributes.

The winter before he died, there was a terrible snowstorm in New York. My dad was making his way home when his car got caught in a snowbank. Along with hundreds of other people that day, he had to abandon his car. Dad ended up walking miles in the freezing cold to get home, and I can't help but wonder if the stress from that day might have kicked off the cancer in his system. There's no way to know for sure.

Later that next year, my dad was admitted to the hospital once again. I remember my mother and I were home one night, and she got a phone call. All they would tell her was that my father had taken a turn for the worse. I think she knew what that meant. We hustled over to the hospital and proceeded to the admissions area. While standing at the desk, my mother stopped cold. In the nearby office she could see a bag sitting near the door, which she immediately recognized as belonging to my father. No one had to say a word. She knew before they told her that my dad had passed away. Then she told me. It was devastating.

I never had enough time with my dad. He was always working, and I was running around doing my stuff. I still miss him and wish he were still around. He never got to see me work, and I think about that from time to time, usually in a quiet moment, standing in an arena somewhere, a couple of hours before game time. I can't help but think, *Man, he would have been really proud.* How I miss him!

When I turned fifty-two not long ago, I thought about my dad a lot, because that was how old he was when he died. I remember when I was a kid thinking that fifty-two was so old! Now I know that he was really young. I know I'm not the only person to lose a parent at a young age. It's part of life. But it was tough.

My dad was the breadwinner, and although my mom worked, mostly at temporary clerical staffing agencies, a "temp" isn't paid that well. We had a house payment and lived in a very expensive city. And, since it was just my mom and me at home now, we both had to do the best we could. She even went back to school and earned her degree at Brooklyn College at the age of fifty-four!

After a few years, my mother advanced into the position of senior vice president of human resources for Chase Manhattan Bank. Basically, the main thrust of her job was helping people do their best. Even though it's obvious by way of her own accomplishments that this lady valued education, she didn't come down too hard on me for cutting class. I think she knew I had found what I wanted to do and was working toward it. She was happy that I had a goal. I think she truly understood why I was going to all these ball games and hanging around and working at radio stations. Or maybe she just got used to it!

My mom probably would have preferred that I didn't skip school. She would ask me, "Don't you have some homework to do?" Usually I would fib and say it was all done. It sounds like another excuse for a kid who didn't want to do his schoolwork, but I really was learning on my own. First of all, I read constantly. I'd go to the corner newsstand every day and get two or three newspapers and read them all the way through. Sports, news, everything. And even though I was a terrible math student, I crunched numbers on my own. I learned fast how to figure out goals against averages. I memorized fielding percentages and the rosters for all the teams. I had a tough time remembering what year the War of 1812 was fought, but I could always tell you Elston Howard's batting average. That's what mattered to me. I knew that if I wanted to be a broadcaster, it was more important to be familiar with a defending team's blue line than the equal sides of an isosceles triangle.

There was one occasion, though, where a nuclear attack wouldn't have kept me from going to school. WPIX, Channel 11 in New York, used to cover the Public School Athletic League (PSAL) high school game of the week every Saturday, and one week they came to my school, Midwood High. All I did that Friday and Saturday was hang around the TV crew and Marty Glickman, the radio Voice of the Knicks and the football Giants, who also did the high school games of the week. I didn't work or help out, although I would have in a heartbeat if they'd asked me. I just watched Glickman's every move as he made his preparations. Here was one of the absolute greats in the business, just an arm's length away! He was really nice; he waved and let me stand nearby as he called the game action in those unmistakable staccato tones.

Years later I learned that Marv Albert (a broadcaster you may have heard of!), who also grew up in Brooklyn, absolutely idolized Glickman when he was a kid. In his book *I'd Love to but I Have a Game*, Albert said that early in his career he tried to imitate Glickman, who became his mentor, even going so far as to put two lumps of sugar in his coffee if that was what Glickman did. He admired Glickman's use of language and the fact that he steered clear from clichés and hype. I was interested to learn that Glickman was an athlete before he became a broadcaster. He was an All-American football player at Syracuse University and was even a teammate of Jesse Owens's on the 1936 U.S. Olympic track team.

But that day on the football field I was thrilled just to be near him. The die was cast; now I really knew what I wanted to do.

If the Yankees or Rangers or Knicks were playing in New York, day or night, I'd do my darnedest to be at the game. In those days, cheap seats were easy to come by, especially when the team wasn't playing well. For sixty cents you could sit in the bleachers at Yankee Stadium, or you could splurge and sit in the upper deck for $1.10. I used to try to pick games where the crowd would be light, and I'd sit way out in the outfield, where nobody else was around, because that way I could bring my little tape recorder, per Bob Wolff's advice, and practice my play-by-play. I realized it must have been terribly annoying to those people sitting near me—not to mention a little strange—to see a kid sitting by himself and talking into a cassette machine. But I was determined to practice. And to do that, I had to go to the game.

Soon it dawned on me that I could get even more practice if I attended games out of town as well. So one day when I went into the city and found out the Rangers were playing in Montreal later that evening, I went to the Port Authority bus terminal, got on a bus, and rode to Montreal.

When the bus stopped at a rest area, I got off and called my mom from the pay phone. (Remember, this was long before cell phones.) I said, "Hi, Mom. I'm going to see the Rangers." She said, "Oh? At the Garden?" I said, "No. In Montreal." I pictured her just shaking her head. "OK, just be careful!"

The prices weren't nearly as expensive as they are today, so I'd buy a ticket from a scalper. I'd watch the game, then as soon as it was over I'd go back to the bus terminal and head home. I did the same thing for a Stanley Cup game in Pittsburgh.

By that time my mom was getting used to my calls.

"Where are you, Eli?"

"Pittsburgh, Mom."

"Pittsburgh? What are you doing in Pittsburgh?"

The Penguins and Bruins were playing that night, and I really wanted to see them play. So I did. After the game I went back to the Pittsburgh bus terminal and rode all night back to New York. The next morning, I'd show back up at the house.

It's not that my mom didn't care where I was. She did. We kept in close touch. I always told her where I was. But she let me be independent, and I appreciated that.

Over the years, I've told this story to my daughter, Elise, who is now a student at the University of Alabama. She would remind me of "the Pittsburgh story" whenever she wanted to make some sort of road trip with her friends or stay out late. But as I told her and still tell her, those were very different times. It was a simpler era. Travel and tickets were a lot cheaper. There weren't the security concerns there are now, and besides, I was on a mission. I wanted to become a broadcaster, and to do this you had to watch a lot of sporting events. As to the skipping-school part of the story, as I've told Elise, it could have all blown up in my face. There was no guarantee I was going to make it. But I was ambitious and passionately felt that I had to take that chance.

THREE

Peanuts! Getcha Peanuts!

EVEN THOUGH THE SEATS WERE RELATIVELY CHEAP BACK IN THE late '60s, a kid could only scare up so much ticket money. So I thought of a way to watch games for free and still make a little cash on the side. I went directly to Madison Square Garden, the new one that had just opened up on Valentine's Day in 1968, and got a job selling peanuts. I was in!

For the next year or two I was basically at the Garden every night. What a magnificent place. This "new" Garden was actually the fourth arena to bear that name. The first two, which opened in 1879 and 1890, respectively, were located at the northeast corner of Madison Square (Madison Avenue and Twenty-sixth Street), hence the buildings' name. The third Garden, which was open to the public from the mid-'20s to the mid-'60s, sat at Fiftieth Street and Eighth Avenue. The new and current Garden, the venue that Pulitzer Prize–winning sportswriter Red Smith called "the most famous and glamorous arena in creation," has staged everything from New York Knicks and Rangers games to the Ali–Frazier fights; both Democratic and Republican Conventions;

hundreds of concerts, from George Harrison's 1971 Concert for Bangledesh to the Concert for New York City following the terrorist attacks of September 11, 2001; and, of course, *WrestleMania*.

The Garden was *the* place to be, and peanuts were my ticket in. As a vendor for the Harry M. Stevens Company, I had an awesome view (I like to refer to it as an "aisle" seat) for big events such as the Millrose Track and Field Games, the Eastern College Athletic Conference (ECAC) Holiday Hockey tournaments, and the National Invitational Tournament (NIT), which in those days featured sixteen teams and was the major college basketball tournament. I also had a great view for dozens of home games for the New York Rangers and the New York Knicks.

I was there in 1969, the year the Knicks—Dick Barnett, Clyde Frazier, and that bunch—won their first league championship. The team started the season strong, winning nine of their first ten games, and kept the momentum going in a year where the center, Willis Reed, won MVP honors for the regular season, the All-Star Game, and the NBA Finals. (This achievement would go unmatched for over two decades until a player named Michael Jordan came along.)

The year 1969 was also when the Rangers, partly energized by their move into a gorgeous new building, compiled ninety-two points during regular-season play and advanced to the play-offs, where they lost to the Bruins in the quarterfinals.

No doubt about it. I was there for the games. I certainly wasn't there for the money. If I had been, I would have sold beer, which was where the big money was. The vendors at the Garden were paid a percentage of what they sold. If percentage was based on a $2.50 can of beer or a $1.50 bag of peanuts (1960s prices), vendors obviously made more money selling beer. I couldn't sell beer, because I was too young. But I didn't want to sell beer anyway.

First of all, the beer trays were really heavy to schlep around.

Peanuts were simple. You carried them in a plastic basket like the one you'd use to carry your dirty laundry down to the washing machine; and when a guy wanted peanuts, you'd throw the bag to him. At the beginning of our shift, the supervisors doled out a certain number of peanuts, and we'd sell them. When all the peanuts were gone, we'd go get another basket.

Even in those days, years before Spike Lee made it an art form, there would be New York politicians, actresses, and actors sitting in the red seats, located in the first few courtside rows. I passed right by Elliott Gould once, making his way to his seat, although he didn't buy any peanuts. The red seats were the good seats, and if you worked in the red seats, those people would give you two dollars for a bag of peanuts that cost a buck and a half and tell you to keep the change. Sometimes they'd give you five dollars! Even so, I didn't want to work the red seats, because when you were down there in the glare of the lights, you really had to work. Therefore I only worked the red seats during the circus—not during any ball games.

Most days, I went up to the blue seats, the cheap seats. I still sold my product, but those people didn't tip. But I could stay up there in the stairways or on the concourse and watch the game while I wandered around doing a halfhearted job selling peanuts. I was still doing my job, because peanuts sort of sell themselves. Everybody likes peanuts. I'd have no trouble unloading the merchandise. But I rarely missed any action on the court or the ice. I'd keep an eye out for any of the bosses who might be nearby, but otherwise I was watching the game. Or the broadcasters in their booth. I'd watch people handing them notes and see them gesturing behind their microphones, and I would think to myself, *That's where I want to be.*

It took me a few months to get up my nerve, but one day I finally ventured up to the offices of the Garden and asked if there was a job available. Bob Wolff, one of the broadcasters I had written a letter to the year before, kept his office there, along with other major muckety-mucks, such as Irving Mitchell Felt, MSG president; Jack Diller, a senior VP; and Alan Rubenstein, the man who would actually hire me. I thought maybe, just maybe, I could get my foot in the door. Mostly due to my low salary expectations (zero), I was hired right away as an office boy for the Madison Square Garden Corporation.

My duties included making coffee, making copies, delivering mail, and hand carrying confidential correspondence between the MSG office and outside law firms. It seems I spent a lot of time taking the bus or subway to deliver contracts or other important documents across town (before the days of FedEx) to the firm of Hunngadunga, Hunngadunga and McCormick on Sixty-eighth and Fifth Avenues. I'd wait for the receptionist to sign for the package; then I'd get back on the bus or the subway, return to the Garden, and get busy with my next task.

I didn't get paid for my work, but I did receive something truly valuable: an employee pass that got me into every single event in Madison Square Garden. It didn't matter whether it was Game Seven of the NBA finals or the Royal Lipizzaner Stallions—now I could get in. Usually I went and hung out in the corner of the press box area behind the green seats, particularly for college events. I had to be a little more flexible during NBA or NHL games, because often all the seats were taken. But I almost always found a place to sit.

While delivering the mail to different professionals in the Garden, one of my regular stops was the office of Ned Irish, who was president of the Knicks. One day, during my regular rounds, his secretary asked, "Are you doing anything this evening, Eli?" I said no. She said, "Well, we have some extra tickets to the Knicks game tonight if you'd like them."

I took her up on her kind offer and a few hours later found myself in the second row, courtside, next to the bench! I had never come down this low before, even when I was selling peanuts. The seats were spectacular. I could actually hear Coach Red Holzman telling his players, "Hit the open man!" I swear I was close enough to feel drops of Dave DeBusschere's sweat.

After that, I always made it a point to swing by Mr. Irish's office, especially when the Knicks were at home. If there was an extra pair of tickets, his secretary, a wonderful lady, would often offer them to me. Sometimes I'd go to the games by myself, or on a rare occasion I'd bring a date. Mostly, I brought one of my friends. Sometimes we'd go to a Knicks game on a Saturday afternoon; then, during the years when the Rangers weren't drawing, if you showed your Knicks ticket later that same night, you could get into the Rangers game for free. So we'd see both games, and in between, we'd kill time at a restaurant called Tad's. We'd get a steak, a baked potato, a piece of Texas toast, a soft drink, and a wilted green salad—not to be confused with the famous wilted spinach salad served at the Hotel 1829 in Saint Thomas. In this case, the wilting was unintentional. Nonetheless, we got all this for eighty-nine cents. That should tell you how good the steak was. Still, my friends and I went there all the time.

For big events sometimes tickets were made available to employees to purchase. One of the biggest events ever was the first Muhammad Ali–Joe Frazier fight, referred to ever after in its hyphenated, Roman-numeraled form, Ali–Frazier I. Because of my job, I had access to the tickets, but they weren't freebies. In fact, they were sold at the unheard-of price of twenty dollars each! For the blue seats! My mom and I hemmed and hawed: "Can we afford this?" I really had to mull it over. As it turned out, my cousin Ira, who was a successful lawyer, ended up buying the tickets and going with me to the fight. I still have the souvenir program with the ticket stapled to it! I'll never forget that night.

In 1971 the introduction of jumbotrons into stadiums and arenas was still years away, but as I remember it, you could see everything clearly. Folks at home watching on their black-and-white TVs couldn't see the color of the spectacle. Here came Ali, bouncing triumphantly into the ring, shadowboxing in his bright crimson-and-white robe, and the crowd cheering and booing all at once—drowning out the PA announcer—as Frazier, decked out in emerald green, made his way down the aisle with his entourage and climbed under the ropes.

Celebrities such as Barbra Streisand, Diana Ross, and Dustin Hoffman took their seats near the ring. Frank Sinatra actually stood on the ring apron, shooting photos for *Life* magazine. There were so many dignitaries and A-listers on hand that even former vice president Hubert Humphrey watched from the balcony—evidently that was the best seat he could get!

From our seats, Ira and I were engrossed in every moment of the bout, which culminated in Frazier's fifteenth-round knockdown of Ali. Like everyone else, including the referee, we were stunned when Ali got up again only to lose the decision to Frazier. Incredible!

Getting the opportunity to attend an event such as this one—not to mention all the games—was a fabulous perk, but probably the best thing about working at the Garden was meeting people such as Bob Wolff, who was doing broadcasts for the Knicks and the Rangers at the time.

Bob Wolff was the big guy in New York! Not only was he the Voice of Madison Square Garden, but he also had a long run as the Voice of the Washington Senators, and later, when the team relocated, the Minnesota Twins. Wolff was the first broadcaster to do the play-by-play of the championships in the four major sports: baseball, football, basketball, and hockey. Among his many accomplishments was broadcasting Don Larsen's perfect game in the 1956 World Series (Yankees vs. Dodgers). This remains the only perfect game in the history of the World Series, and Wolff's voice—"Strike three! A no-hitter, a perfect game for Don Larsen!"—is forever attached to it!

Another big game forever linked with Bob Wolff is the 1958 NFL Championship Game between the New York Giants and the Baltimore Colts, sometimes referred to as "The Greatest Game Ever Played." Trivia buffs may be interested to know that Wolff's spotter—an assistant who points things out to the play-by-play announcer during the broadcast—for this broadcast was a young college student named Maury Povich.

I once heard a story that when he was a very young man, Wolff made a list of all the famous people he wanted to meet. If I had made such a list, at that point, Bob Wolff would have topped it. Not only did I meet him, but he went on to play an enormous role in my development.

Whenever I got the chance, I'd use my employee pass to get into hockey or basketball games, and find a seat, preferably off by myself, and practice my play-by-play. Once I had compiled a few tapes, I stopped by Bob Wolff's office and asked his secretary—I think her name was Ellie—if she thought it would be all right to ask her boss to critique one of my tapes. She told me she didn't think this would be a problem at all.

I got up my nerve, and the next day I asked Bob Wolff to listen to one of my tapes and critique my work. And he did this for me! He played the tape while I was standing there and told me, "Work on this . . . This isn't bad here . . . Next time do this . . ." The one comment I remember clearly is when he told me to slow down. He also suggested I give the time and the score more frequently throughout my "broadcast." I still hear that comment to this day!

From that point forward, I always made sure to have a tape with me just in case I ran into Bob. And as I recall, some of those tapes were awful. I mean, abysmal! But he really cared; he listened to these dreadful things and took me seriously. I'll always be grateful to him for that. This was incredible to me. Here was the guy who called

Don Larsen's perfect game on TV, giving *me* advice. A Hall of Famer! You'd better believe I listened to him.

Another guy I used to run into during my stint as a boy Friday was a young broadcaster named Marv Albert. He had just taken over Marty Glickman's job as the radio Voice of the Knicks, and sometimes I'd go stand around when he was working, like the geeky kid I was. I'd always keep a respectful distance, but one time I couldn't resist going up to him and telling him I wanted his job. He was another one of the guys I had written an "advice" letter to, and his response was priceless. First, he apologized for not writing back sooner! Then, he advised me to read as much as possible, both sports and nonsports subjects. (Done.) He also suggested I attend, watch, and listen to as many sporting events as possible. (Done.) And his parting words to me were, "Above all, do not neglect your studies." (Sorry, Marv.)

Flash forward: At the end of the 2008 NFL season, while attending the Titans game in Nashville, I visited the broadcast booth prior to kickoff. Albert was there doing the national radio broadcast, so I went over and introduced myself. I said, "Marv, I'm not sure if you remember me, but when I was a teenager, I used to go up and see you in the booth at the Garden all the time."

Well, either he was being polite or he really did remember, because he said, "Oh, yeah!" I then told him I didn't mean to imply that he was old by saying I was a teenager when our paths first crossed some forty years ago. I didn't want to offend one of my heroes. Not that I would ever dare to compare myself to Albert, but there are some parallels in that we were both young guys growing up in Brooklyn who wanted to do the exact same thing. Albert used to pretend to be sick (evidently he can sneeze on command) so he could stay home from school and listen to ball games on the radio. He and his brothers created their own make-believe radio station, WMPA, named for Marv Philip Aufrichtig. (He later changed his last name to Albert.) The brothers called everything on their station, from high school games, to stuff going on outside their window, to the Gerbil Olympics, which they staged themselves.

Albert was a teenage panelist on one of Howard Cosell's early ventures, *All-League Clubhouse*, a weekly show where a sports guest took questions from kids. He then worked as an office boy for the Brooklyn Dodgers, a job that included changing the numbers on the manual scoreboard on top of the Dodgers' office building. In his book *I'd Love to but I Have a Game*, Albert describes shimmying through the crawl space and squeezing through a crevice to get to the roof, where he would listen to Vin Scully's radio broadcast to keep track of the score. He also confesses to once putting up the wrong score because he couldn't find the number 7.

Albert first made his way into the Garden as a ball boy for the Knicks. He was also their fan club president and put out a newsletter called "Knick Knacks," which helped him score a gig doing stats for Marty Glickman, who became his champion. Albert used to practice calling games into Glickman's reel-to-reel and eventually got his big break when he succeeded him doing the broadcast.

Everybody knows that Albert has gone on to do numerous sports for multiple outlets. I think he is one of the best broadcasters in the history of the world. His abilities are par excellence. He has gotten to where he is because he deserves it. He works hard, his pacing is fabulous, and perhaps most important, he has that innate talent of being able to see something and describe it instantly. Even to this day, if I hear him on the radio, it stops me in my tracks. I will listen to him even if it's a game I don't care about. On a God-given side, there's just a quality to his voice that captures you. When you hear that voice, there is no question that you are listening to Marv Albert. You're not going to confuse him with Al Michaels or Bob Costas! He has a sportscaster's voice that's unique, and there's nothing like being unique!

Marv Albert would still be a Hall of Fame broadcaster even without the Marv Albert voice. This is true of many of the greats. I mean, you can't sound like Elmer Fudd and call play-by-play for a living. You have to have some semblance of a listenable voice. Although when it comes to color analysts, there is a little more leeway. For instance, former Crimson Tide color man Kenny Stabler and NASCAR's Buddy Baker do not have classic voices, but they are champions and bring something to the table that far usurps tonal quality. But play-by-play guys need to develop a talent for describing what they see along with the ability to string a few sentences together. Combine that with a spectacular set of pipes, and you have something great. Like Marv Albert.

FOUR

This Ain't a One-Hour Television Spectacular!

AROUND THE TIME I WAS DELIVERING MAIL, SHADOWING BROAD-casters, and catching games at the Garden, I heard through one of the guys at WOR that the Mutual Broadcasting System was looking for audio engineers. All those days I spent hanging around radio stations turned out to be productive, because I actually received some great training. I had just enough experience to start out at the entry level.

I was on my way to my first real radio job.

If you look back at old newsreels and news photos of U.S. presidents at press conferences over the years, you will probably find a large microphone at the podium with a big flag that says "Mutual." Without a doubt, Mutual was the leading radio network back in its day, and since I had been an intern at WOR, a big Mutual affiliate, I had an edge when they were hiring. So I got the job—this time a paying gig—and worked the morning shift for a year or so.

When I say "morning," I mean early morning. Most days I'd get up and take the subway into Manhattan from Brooklyn, arriving at the network around 4:30 a.m. Sure, at that hour it was a little spooky riding the train into the city. But I rode the subway all the time; a lot of kids my age did. In fact, I remember seeing Marv Albert's younger brothers, Al and Steve, on the D-train many times. You have to remember, it was an entirely different era. Of course, I had to be careful. I wasn't a stupid kid. I'd ride in the car with the conductor or in the car where the policeman was stationed, and I never had a problem. You could improve your odds if you used some common sense.

The thing was, I really, really wanted to be there. I was engineering morning newscasts and doing news feeds for Bob Considine, a noted commentator whom I would describe as the Andy Rooney of his day. Besides his radio gig, Considine was also a prolific author known best for his books, including *Thirty Seconds over Tokyo* and *The Babe Ruth Story*. Legend had it that he worked on two typewriters at once: one for news stories, one for his book in progress—although I never confirmed that firsthand. What I knew for sure was that I was learning heaps of practical skills and being paid very well. Union wages were about $356 a week, not bad money in 1968, especially for a fifteen-year-old kid living at home.

Getting up at three in the morning was rough. What teenager wants to get out of bed at that ungodly hour? But it was a small price to pay for my dream job. The early shift worked for me because I could work for a few hours, and on the rare occasions I did go to school, I could actually get there before the second bell. Oftentimes, though, I would stay and work through the morning and into the afternoon shift. I just couldn't get enough of the broadcasting business.

Occasionally, when I was working in the middle of a weekday, an adult would say to me, "Hey, aren't you supposed to be in school?" The thing was, there were so many high school–age kids in New York when I was growing up that they had to stagger the hours of the school day. Kids went to school in shifts, either from 7:00 to 11:00 a.m.,

11:00 a.m. to 3:00 p.m., or 3:00 to 7:00 p.m. So, if it was early morning, I'd say I didn't have to be in school until later. If it was late, I'd say I went early. After a while people got used to seeing me around on school days. For the most part, people didn't ask questions. As far as they were concerned, I was working and behaving myself. In New York, people tended to mind their own business.

The job with Mutual put me in contact with some incredible talents, including Dell Sharbutt and Marvin Scott, longtime announcers who did news and commentary. I often ran the board for Fred Foy, a Mutual staff announcer best remembered as the narrator on the radio series of *The Lone Ranger*. I still love that series! Even today, when making a long car trip, I'll while away the hours listening to shows like *Dragnet*, *The Shadow*, or *The Lone Ranger* on the RadioClassics channel (118) on Sirius Satellite Radio.

Back in my engineering days, I often found myself just on the other side of the glass from some of the best-known voices of the day. As staff announcers, these men would come in and tape a whole week's worth of "ins and outs," the audio that serves as the segue in and out of a particular program. They'd approach the mic and say, "Tonight, Bob Considine talks with David Suskind at six o'clock . . . Tonight, Bob Considine talks with David Suskind at seven o'clock . . . at eight o'clock . . ." (Different times for different time zones.)

For the most part, broadcasters still work this way (minus the cassette tapes). While doing promos for the Motor Racing Network (MRN), I'll say, "Hi, everybody, this is Eli Gold! Join me on Tuesday night at seven o'clock . . . Tuesday night at six o'clock . . . Tuesday night at five o'clock . . . where our guest will be Tony Stewart, right here on *NASCAR Live!*" The only difference is that, back then, they would send out a cassette or a reel-to-reel tape to affiliates in different regions of the country for them to use through the week. These days, we send the promos out digitally or via satellite.

It wasn't long before my job at Mutual Broadcasting led to an opportunity to work as a "relief" audio engineer for the ABC radio networks. I joined the union, NABET Local 16 (National Association of Broadcast Engineers and Technicians), and began filling in for engineers who were on vacation. And somebody was always on vacation.

ABC had several different networks at the time. There was the Information Network, the Entertainment Network, the American Contemporary Network, and the FM Network, all of which fed programming to different-formatted radio stations. I filled in wherever I was needed.

I ran the board for several big-name broadcasters at ABC, including Bill Diehl, Bob Hardt, Bob Walker, and Don Gardiner, who had the distinction of being the first radio announcer in the country to report that President Kennedy had been shot in Dallas on November 22, 1963.

Not all of the announcers were old hands, though. For example, I engineered the very first newscast for a reporter named Ann Compton, who had just started her career with ABC. I remember her being a little on edge prior to the first show, but she was still solid. Soon after that, Compton was assigned to cover the White House and has since covered seven presidents as the national correspondent for ABC radio. Every once in a while I'll see her on TV—I'm one of these weird guys who watches C-SPAN, especially if they are televising a White House correspondent's dinner or a media roundtable at the Overseas Press Club—as the emcee of the event. Of course, I take full credit for her success!

The most memorable ABC gig for me, though, was when I engineered the broadcast of Howard Cosell's longtime daily sportscast *Speaking of Sports*.

When I began engineering his program, Cosell was already a household name. I loved listening to him on *Monday Night Football*, which was on TV very late. I remember my mom coming in and saying, "You've got to go to bed!"

The majority of the time, Cosell's partners on the broadcast were former football stars Frank Gifford and Don Meredith. The public especially loved the combination and the frequent clashes between the down-to-earth, folksy Meredith and the more intellectual, caustic Cosell. Years later, Cosell coined the term *jockocracy* to describe the trend of putting former athletes in the broadcast booth. He made no secret of his disdain of this practice.

Bob Uecker, a not-so-successful jock turned super-successful broadcaster, told a story in the book *Storytellers* about a run-in he had with Cosell. According to Uecker, while on the air with him once, Cosell used the word *truculent*. He turned to Uecker and said, "Since you're a former player, you couldn't possibly know the meaning of that word." Uecker didn't skip a beat. "I sure do," he said. "If you had a truck and I borrowed it, that would be a truck you lent."

As a play-by-play guy, I have a great respect for color analysts who have played the game. As I've said many times about Kenny Stabler, my longtime color man for the University of Alabama broadcasts, he brought something to the table that I never could. I've never even taken a snap in football, let alone won a Super Bowl. So I valued his perspective immensely. I consider myself a describer. Former players or coaches who have been there and done that? Invaluable.

No question, Cosell had his opinions, and in my humble opinion, he was welcome to them. People either loved him or hated him. A 1978 *TV Guide* poll—and probably dozens of others in previous and subsequent years—listed him as both the most-loved and most-hated broadcaster in America. He was the first guy who really told it like it was. In fact, "I'm just telling it like it is" became his catchphrase. He had the guts to speak out, and he took some controversial stands, such as defending Muhammad Ali when the heavyweight champ refused to be inducted into the military during the Vietnam War. I always thought that was such a fascinating dynamic, watching Ali, a newly initiated Black Muslim from Louisville, Kentucky, mesh so well with Cosell, a white Jewish guy from Brooklyn.

Whether you agreed or disagreed with him, no one could deny that Cosell was incredibly special. He was not just a sportscaster but more of a linguist and a wordsmith. What a magnificent vocabulary!

His approach was more akin to something you'd expect from a hard news reporter than a sports guy. Some even went so far as to call him "the Edward R. Murrow of sportscasting."

Although Cosell is forever thought of as a New Yorker, Howard William Cohen (he changed his name in college) was actually born in Winston-Salem, North Carolina, in 1918. Soon after, his family moved to Brooklyn, where he was raised. Although he showed some interest in sports journalism early on as sports editor of his high school paper, he went on to get a degree from the New York University School of Law and practiced law briefly after serving in World War II. Then, after spending three years hosting a program for ABC Radio for one of his clients, the Little League of New York, he made the switch and began pursuing a full-time broadcasting career. By the mid-'50s, Cosell was on staff at ABC and quickly made a name for himself as a guy who didn't pull any punches when he teamed with ex-Brooklyn Dodgers pitcher Ralph Branca for WABC's pre- and postgame broadcasts for the New York Mets.

When I engineered Cosell's show, most days I literally never saw him. Although he sometimes came into the studio, most of the time Cosell recorded *Speaking of Sports*, his daily five-minute afternoon show, from his home in Pound Ridge, New York. Nowadays, it's commonplace for broadcasters to have studios in their homes. I have a studio in my home in Birmingham and at our beach house in Ocean Isle Beach, North Carolina. In fact, these days most radio talk-show hosts originate programs from their homes. But back in the late '60s and early '70s, this was a huge deal. You had to be a megastar to have what in those days was called a "dry pair," an actual pair of wires that ran from your home through the phone company toll test board, then all the way to the network headquarters. If you had that set-up, you knew you were big. And Howard Cosell was big.

ABC had state-of-the-art equipment. All we had to do from our end was punch up a code into the board that activated the switch to Cosell's house in Pound Ridge. That's how it was labeled: "Pound Ridge." Turning on the switch was one of my responsibilities.

You never wanted Cosell to be waiting around for you, so if we recorded the show at 4:00 p.m., at about 3:30 p.m. we activated the gear from New York City. Then, we would listen. Not eavesdropping, per se, but in order to be ready, we had to listen. And we always rolled tape, just in case.

To this day I still have some of those tapes. I don't play them for anyone, and I won't! But there are some amazing reels. I have some great tapes of Howard Cosell singing, including one of my favorites, a complete rendition of "For Once in My Life." Instead of Sinatra, it's Cosell singing, "For once in my life, I won't let sorrow hurt me, not like it's hurt me before . . ."

On the air the guy was spectacular. The few times I saw him in the studio, the first thing I noticed was that he came in with no notes. He just sat down and started doing this magnificent show without a single written word in front of him! What an incredible brain. He really knew his stuff.

Now that I am a broadcaster myself, the thing I probably admire most about him was his clock. Broadcasters all have an imaginary clock in their heads. I make my wife a little crazy sometimes. She'll say, "What time is it?" and I'll answer, "It's got to be about 2:17." Then she'll say, "Why can't you just say, 'a quarter after two,' like normal people?" It's a habit because exact timing is essential in our line of work.

Cosell's sense of timing was absolutely perfect. He would do that show—five minutes with the commercial—without looking at the clock. He'd craft this masterful commentary all in his head, and at exactly four minutes and fifty eight seconds into his show, he'd say, "This is Howard Cosell reporting." Unbelievable.

Another thing Cosell had going for him was his one-of-a-kind voice. From his first word, you knew you were listening to Howard Cosell. That's an enviable commodity to have in the broadcasting business. His nasally, herky-jerky Brooklyn sound turned out to be a big bonus. Distinctive voices are often what make a good broadcaster an extraordinary broadcaster.

Then there was his approach. Direct. Opinionated. Outspoken. Even though it sometimes came off as haughty or even arrogant, Cosell legitimized this type of reporting. Whether you liked him or not, you tuned in to hear what he was going to say next. No doubt about it, his "tell it like it is" methodology revolutionized sports broadcasting.

In many regards, Cosell's on-air and off-air personas were similar. I remember one day he came into the ABC building and stopped in the lobby at a cigar stand, as he often did. Most people would walk up and say, "Hey! Whatcha got?" Cosell would say, "Have you got a cigar worth my smoking?" In other words, he turned it around as if the cigar should be honored to be slipping between his lips.

I guess he earned a little arrogance, although I have to say, it made me sad to see him turn bitter in his later years. I didn't see him much after those few early encounters, except from a distance, and if I had, he wouldn't have known me from Adam's house cat. Back then I was just a kid who got his show on the air. I hardly talked to him directly. Mostly I'd say to the producer, "I need a level." Then the producer would say, "Howard, we need a level." Then Cosell would say, "Hello again, everyone . . . ," and we'd get our audio level.

Basically, I was the guy running the board and carrying the equipment. As an engineer, my goal was to not be noticed. I wanted to fly under the radar. I never wanted to screw up on any job, but I especially didn't want to mess up while I was working for Cosell.

There was that one time, though. We were a minute or two into the show, and Cosell was on a roll, talking without a script and doing an absolutely brilliant commentary. Right in the middle of it, I accidentally hit a button, triggering a commercial, and he was forced to stop. Before we regrouped and started over, he turned and looked right at me and said, "It's a simple radio show. This ain't a one-hour television spectacular."

He didn't yell. He didn't curse. But in typical broadcaster style— instead of making an economical comment—"Hey! C'mon, kid!"— he chose to string together two sentences punctuated at the end with a four-syllable word.

Great, great stuff.

Of course, as an up-and-coming young engineer, I did more than push a few buttons. In addition to my training as an audio engineer, I also learned how to edit tape. These days, editing is done on computers; but back in those days, you used tape—actual recording tape— and when you wanted to make a change, you edited with a grease pencil and a razor blade.

First, you'd cue up the tape. Then you'd run it back and forth at a slow speed. Then when you found the spot you were looking for— the end of a breath, the end of a word—you'd take a grease pencil and make a mark on the tape. Not on the side that held the audio but the other side. Then you would put the tape on an editing block, line it up along these little serrated edges, take a razor blade, and make your cut. You'd physically cut the tape. There was your sound bite, a piece of audiotape you could literally hold in your hand.

Sometimes I messed up and had to either piece the tape back together or accept the fact that my mistake had hit the cutting-room floor. Literally. It took plenty of practice, but eventually I could edit tape in my sleep.

These days, I edit audio files on my laptop. First, I access what are called *wave files*. Then I find the beginning and end of the sound bite I'm looking for and pull it out electronically. This is easier and better than the ol' slice-and-dice in so many ways. For one thing, if you make a mistake, the original file is still on your hard drive. Plus, you can work on the road. I often find myself on an airplane with my laptop open and headphones stuck in my ears, editing an interview I did at one track so that I can use it in two weeks during the race at another track. And perhaps most important, editing on a laptop is much less cumbersome than how we did it in the old days. Not only is the cut-and-paste element obsolete, but I no longer have to travel with tons of heavy stuff.

Even the great Howard Cosell used to schlep his enormous reel-to-reel tape recorder (housed in an even bigger case) from ballpark to ballpark to get his interviews in the '50s, '60s, and '70s. (Maybe that partly explains his sometimes-cantankerous demeanor?)

The same held true for future NASCAR executives. The first time I met Mike Helton, who is now president of NASCAR, he was still climbing the ranks as a young sportscaster at WOPI radio in Bristol, Tennessee, and we were both working at Bristol International Raceway, now known as the Bristol Motor Speedway. At the time, there were no escalators or elevators at the track. When Mike arrived, hauling a giant suitcase of equipment up a towering grandstand, the sweat was flying!

I guess you could call that the sportscaster's equivalent of walking ten miles in the snow to get to school.

It builds character. But I for one am thrilled that these days I can literally do an entire broadcast from my laptop computer.

Along with my engineering jobs and other paying gigs, such as selling peanuts, I continued to take on as many part-time jobs and internships as I could manage. It didn't matter to me if they paid anything, as long as I could attend sporting events or was learning about broadcasting. So I kept logging time at WOR and WNEW and even worked awhile as an audio engineer at a Spanish-language television station— WNJU in Newark, New Jersey. *Usted nunca sabe cuando va a tener su grande opportunidad!* (You never know where you're going to get your big break!)

Then, it happened. And as important a milestone as it was to me, I can't remember the particulars of my first day on the air. My hazy recollection is that one day, one of many I spent working at Mutual, someone called in sick. Since I had mentioned my on-air aspirations to more than a few people, I was pressed into service. It must have been Scotty Morrison, the sports director at the time, who said, "Hey! Do you think you can do a minute and a half at 10:40 this morning and not screw it up?"

Heck, yeah!

Predictably enough, my first on-air report sounded like it was coming out of the mouth of a kid who was scared out of his wits. Because that's exactly what I was. And my next report probably sounded pretty much the same.

I was soon "promoted" to stringer, which means I got the chance to be an on-the-scene correspondent, sending back live reports from ball games. This job was not prestigious. I didn't get paid. In fact, I was so low on the totem pole that I wasn't even issued a press pass, which would have gotten me into the game for free. Basically, when I went to Jets games, I called in reports.

In those days there were no cell phones, but at Shea Stadium there was a pay phone near my seat out on the concourse. Before we left for the game, I made sure I had plenty of change. Then, once every quarter or so, I would call in and give my fifteen-second quickie update, the kind you still hear today on a fast-paced sports show. The cool thing was that I got to give the report live, on the air. I didn't just call in to relay the information to someone at the station. It was my voice on the radio! The sports director may have questioned the wisdom of this decision, though, when during a certain Broncos–Jets game I said, "Joe Namath just completed a 12-yard touchdown pass to Don Maynard after a Broncos touchdown score by Billy Odoms . . ." (The problem was, the player's name was *Riley* Odoms.)

As I learned quickly, when that happens, you just keep going. ". . . and the score is Jets 14, Broncos 7."

Over the next few years I continued to work as a stringer as often as possible. Often, it was a matter of my volunteering to cover a game and the bosses saying, "Sure kid. Go ahead. As long as it doesn't cost us anything."

Then, late in 1971, I went down to Hollywood, Florida, to visit my aunt Pearl and uncle Harry. Since Hollywood is just a few miles north of Miami, I generously volunteered to cover the Dolphins game for Mutual while I was down there. I got the OK, and this time I was paid twenty dollars and, more important, was issued a press pass. For a game at the Orange Bowl! Over the years I have heard broadcasters poke gentle and not-so-gentle fun at the working conditions at the Orange Bowl, which have deteriorated over the years.

But when I walked in there in the early '70s, the year the Super Bowl–bound Dolphins won the AFC East (they lost to the Cowboys in the Super Bowl, 24-3) and saw the likes of Don Shula, Larry Csonka, and Bob Griese down on the field, man, I felt like I was walking into the Taj Mahal!

To me, this was the greatest thing in the world. The job was easy enough. All I had to do was call back to the Mutual studios at halftime and again after the game and give them a brief thirty-to-forty-second telephone update. It's hard to imagine that this was the mode of communication then, but there was no Internet, and not all games were on TV in those days.

The game was the highlight of my trip to the Sunshine State. I wasn't much for the beach, and I'm sure my aunt and uncle thought I was nuts because I kept disappearing into the guest bedroom every hour on the hour to listen to the Mutual newscasts on the local Miami station. I visualized what was going on back in New York—they were probably loading tapes, pushing this button or that button. Then, after the newscast, I'd go back out and rejoin my aunt and uncle. I remember telling my uncle, who worked much of his life in a handbag factory, about working at the Dolphins game.

"Nobody makes money doing that," he said. In fact, years later, my aunt Stella, who is in her late seventies, still doesn't believe I make money going to sporting events. "You mean they pay you for this?"

Back then, it was even hard for me to imagine someday making a living by watching and talking about sports. But I just kept at it. Not long after my trip to Miami, I volunteered to cover a game at the Houston Astrodome. Again, I paid my own way. And once again, I think I made twenty dollars in addition to getting a press pass into the game.

Some people didn't care for the atmosphere in the Astrodome, but I remember walking in there and saying out loud, "Holy crap! I'm in the Astrodome!" I felt as though I was walking into St. Peter's Basilica in Rome. I didn't think about the fact that I had to park in the overflow parking lot instead of in the media lot, up close. I didn't care about where my seat was. There was a game going on, and I was there.

FIVE

Don't Blow it

ALTHOUGH SEVERAL BROADCASTERS I ADMIRED AND HOPED TO emulate had gotten their sheepskins from excellent communications schools such as Syracuse University or the University of Missouri, I had long determined that I was never going to learn how to call balls and strikes on the air by sitting in a classroom. A formal college education was simply not in the cards for me. The primary reason being that I barely got out of high school.

First of all, I was absent more days than I was present. My teachers had long grown accustomed to not seeing me, and I really didn't get in trouble because my mom knew that I was working. So, toward the end of my senior year, my mother approached my high school principal, whom she knew from way back when he was her high school social studies teacher. She told him, "Look, he's a good boy. He knows what he wants to do. Give him his diploma, and he won't bother anybody."

The principal agreed. As part of the deal, I didn't walk across the stage at my high school graduation. I wasn't upset about it. In fact,

I'm pretty sure I was working that night. I was more than ready to move on.

Still, as unexpected as it was, I had a brief flirtation with a college education. While working as an intern at WOR in New York as a teen-

ager, I got to know John Gambling, the host of *Rambling with Gambling*, the number one morning show in the country. His son was a student at Boston University and also worked as operations manager of WTBU, the school's student radio station. Somehow, through John Gambling's connections, I was accepted at BU.

In August, just two months after my pseudo–high school graduation, I went to Boston and checked in at school. My dorm was right on Kenmore Square on Commonwealth

Yes, I once had dark hair.

Avenue. From the roof you could look down and see Fenway Park, which was only a block and a half away. As a Yankees fan, I hated that!

The radio station, located in the Myles Standish Building, was just a short walk away from the dorm, so my first day in town I went there and immediately started work. I did a little bit of everything, and I was soon thrown into the deep end doing live, on-air sportscast-ing. I still have some of those tapes hidden away, and they are bad. I talked way too fast in this terrible, high-pitched voice. I mean, I sounded awful! But you have to start somewhere.

I worked at the station every day. Oftentimes I'd be working along-side other aspiring broadcasters, including George Schweitzer, who went on to become the marketing group president for CBS. A bunch of us used to go eat lunch and dinner together all the time at the sub shop next door, which we affectionately called "Filthies."

In the evening, I would often go watch games and practice my play-by-play at the Boston Garden, where the Boston Braves, a minor-league team in the American Hockey League, used to play. I also brought my tape recorder to as many BU sporting events as possible and practiced there too. The one thing I didn't do was go to class. Ever.

In high school, at least I showed up every once in a while. But I may have been the first student in BU's history to literally never cross the threshold of a classroom. The radio station was my classroom. I learned a ton of practical skills and made some great contacts. But it didn't take long to figure out that this wasn't going to work for the long haul. I couldn't let my mom pay tuition so I could be a resident of a dorm and work at a radio station; therefore I left school.

Once I got back to New York, I returned to Madison Square Garden and assumed my duties as the kid who would do anything. But it wasn't long before I would be less available for errands and making copies, because that year, I was offered my first on-air job. The Rangers? The Knicks? Let's not get ahead of ourselves. Still, I was thrilled to be named the new color commentator for the Long Island Ducks.

The Ducks (est. 1959) were in the Eastern Hockey League, a minor pro hockey league, who played at the Long Island Arena (also known as the Commack Arena) from 1954 to 1973. By the time I hooked on with the Ducks, the league consisted of teams from cities such as New Haven, Jacksonville, Nashville, and Roanoke, to name a few.

In 1971 Ducks games were broadcast on a very low-powered radio station, WRCN, in Riverhead, New York, which is all the way on the eastern end of Long Island. These were low-impact broadcasts with a very small listening audience; the games couldn't be heard very far from the station. Still, I jumped at the offer to become their color man. As it turned out, I only did the color commentary for two games.

Within a week the regular play-by-play guy left the team, and I moved into the play-by-play chair. I felt as though I had arrived.

At our first meeting, Al Baron, the team owner and a local businessman who also owned South Bay Electric Company, told me that he would pay all my expenses for the season. I really appreciated this since I would be commuting to Long Island from Brooklyn and didn't have a car. No one had a car. You didn't need one in New York. I used to take the subway to the Long Island Railroad, get off in Northport, then take a cab to the arena, which was cheaper than owning a car and fussing with parking in the city. But still, train tickets and cabs cost money, so I was glad to have my expenses covered. Mr. Baron also agreed to pay for my hotels and meals when I traveled with the team—I got the same six-dollar meal money that everyone else did—and I was especially glad about that.

Regarding salary, Mr. Baron said, "At the end of the year, I'll take care of you." I took that to mean I'd get some sort of compensation. True to his word, at the end of the season, Mr. Baron shook my hand and presented me with an envelope. Inside was my season's pay: a fifty-dollar Sear's gift certificate.

Knowing me, I probably went over to Sear's and swapped the certificate for another tape recorder. Regardless, I don't remember being terribly disappointed with my "salary." In reality, my pay for that first year was the opportunity to do play-by-play for fifty or sixty games on radio. I was working and I was learning, and I was improving every day. My job with the Ducks allowed me to ride the bus with the team and see new places. Most important, I had my first "real" radio job.

The first game I called was in Syracuse, New York. The Ducks were playing the Syracuse Blazers at the Onondaga County War Memorial Auditorium. I was thankful that my first game was on the road, because I figured that regardless of what I said, if I said it clearly, it was going to sound accurate on the radio. If I missed any plays or passes—and I did—I didn't want anybody attending the game to turn on a radio and compare the game action to what I was saying, because at times, it didn't match.

I was in good company that night. The Voice of the Syracuse Blazers was Andy MacWilliams, a great broadcaster who also did the Jacksonville Barons games in the American Hockey League and later went on to do Cincinnati Reds baseball on WLW in Cincinnati. When MacWilliams left Syracuse, a young guy named Bob Costas took over for him.

Hockey night in Hampton, Va.

Costas was a New York guy, born in Queens. He grew up in Commack, New York, the town where the Long Island Ducks played their games. After graduating from Commack High School, he attended Syracuse University; and while still a student there, he was hired as the Voice of the Syracuse Blazers hockey team, even though he'd only previously attended two hockey games! Incredibly, he won the job by submitting a tape of his Syracuse basketball game broadcast.

As millions of people now know, Costas' first love is baseball. In his eloquent way, he tells stories about turning the dial on his father's car radio when he was a kid, trying to "eavesdrop" on a baseball game in faraway towns such as Baltimore, Cincinnati, or, on a clear night, St. Louis. He also admits to crying the first time he visited Yankee Stadium. Evidently, he walked out to center field after the game, where at the time there was a flagpole and monuments to Babe Ruth, Lou Gehrig, and Miller Huggins. Young Costas mistakenly thought this was the Yankees' burial ground and was overcome with emotion. But since he was only seven at the time, we'll give him a break.

Back in the early '70s, we were both aspiring broadcasters working our first play-by-play gigs for different teams in the Eastern Hockey League. One afternoon, prior to a Ducks–Blazers game, Bob and I got together for lunch. Since our palettes, not to mention our wallets, were less than developed at the time, we decided to take our luncheon meeting at the White Castle burger joint, which wasn't far from my hotel. As we made our way along the main street in Syracuse, Bob and I began calling the play-by-play of ourselves walking down the street.

"Costas goes to the left, Gold to the right! They make the move around the fire hydrant and back onto the sidewalk . . ." When we reached the White Castle, I probably described the building's white, Medieval castle–like exterior, while Bob certainly commented that the fast-food restaurant's crenellated tower was reminiscent of Chicago's Water Tower.

Then, with our respective bags of those small, greasy, square Slyders (hamburgers) in hand, we went back down the street. "Costas moves out ahead; he's through the door. But Gold is keeping pace . . ."

It wasn't long before Bob submitted that same Syracuse basketball tape to a radio station in St. Louis, KMOX, and at age twenty-two was hired as the Voice of the Spirits of St. Louis of the now-defunct American Basketball Association.

A few years later, Bob and I once again found ourselves working the same hockey game, this time covering the same team. I had been hired to do the TV broadcast for the NHL's St. Louis Blues, while the legendary Dan Kelly was doing the radio broadcasts. Sometimes Kelly would have a scheduling conflict, since he was also the radio Voice of the St. Louis Cardinals football team (before they moved to Arizona), so KMOX would bring in Bob to fill in on the hockey games.

So, here we were, prior to game time one Sunday at the old Montreal Forum, where the visiting team's radio and TV booths were literally side by side, separated only by a tiny wall. We were both thirty seconds from going on the air, when Bob Costas leaned around the skinny wall from his radio booth, stuck his head into the TV booth, and said, "Young Eli, tonight you will have one of your largest audiences ever, because once America hears that it's me doing the play-by-play on the radio, trust me, they will all turn to television."

I'm sure Bob called a great game—he is superb at everything—but he probably felt, especially back then, that hockey was not his best sport. It's not his baseball. Nevertheless, here was the guy who went on to do every major sporting event—the Olympics, the World Series, the Super Bowl—with a few pregame jitters.

"Don't blow it!" He laughed, then sat back down and began his broadcast.

After the game that night, exiting onto St. Catherine's Street in snowy Montreal, I said, "How'd ya do?"

Bob said, "This was the very best game that Francois Ouimet ever played."

I was confused at first. "Why is that?" I asked.

"Because," Bob said, "whenever I didn't know who the player was, I said it was Francois Ouimet."

In fact, Ouimet was a real guy. It wasn't like Bob kept calling him Jubilee Dunbar. But he had Ouimet on the ice for some fifty minutes that night!

Over the years, our paths have crossed many times. In February one year, I was in Daytona during NASCAR's Speed Weeks and he was working the NBA All-Star game in Orlando. We had talked about getting together, so one evening I called him at his hotel to finalize our plans.

He answered the phone. I said, "Costy, Eli here!"

He said, "Young Eli, let me tell you what an inopportune moment this is. I stand here, dripping wet, having just stepped out of the shower. I have you on this phone line, Dick Ebersol on the other, and the room service waiter, who is none too tentative with his banging, is at my door. May I call you back?"

Now, that's a true sportscaster. He could have said, "I'll call you back." But why economize? Why say something in three or four words when you can say it in three or four sentences? He can't help himself.

Kidding aside, no one is better with words than Costas. First of all, he has the closest thing to a photographic memory I've ever seen. But what blows me away is the language he uses. Every word he uses is chosen carefully, has a purpose, and accomplishes something.

I was at home one night, watching Costas hosting NBC's coverage of the Olympics. On the program, Bud Collins, a tennis expert, was interviewing a competitor who said she was distracted during her match because her home country had just undergone an attempted coup earlier that day. They discussed this for a few minutes—how the insurgents came in and there was some violence—and she was worried about family back home.

The cameras came back to Costas, who said, "Thank you, Bud. A remarkable interview. Please tell Natalia that we checked, and the insurgents only got as far as the state-run radio station before they were turned back. Further good news, the only damage they were able to inflict at the station was changing the format from country music to urban contemporary."

I sat straight up and said, "My God! What a magnificent line!"

Sure, obviously Bob had a little research assistance from the NBC staff, who no doubt worked furiously to get an update while the interview was still in progress. But with his gift for turning a phrase, Bob delivered the serious news that the coup had been foiled while using his quick wit to leave the segment on an upbeat note! Incredible.

I'll never forget the time during the 1979 hockey season when my wife, Claudette, finally met Bob. She'd heard stories about him and heard me talking to him on the phone over the years, but I suspect she was just the slightest bit starstruck during their first meeting.

It was in Atlanta; I was doing the St. Louis Blues game that night against the Atlanta Flames at the Omni Arena, while Bob was doing the Chicago Bulls game for WGN in Chicago. They were to meet the Atlanta Hawks at the Omni the next night. We met after the hockey game at a Chinese restaurant in the building that is now the CNN Center. We all sat down and ordered a couple of toddies. Claudette leaned over to me and said, "Bob's a good-looking man. I can see why a woman would think he's attractive."

And to Bob she said, "It's great to meet you." And a few minutes later she said, "It sure is great to meet you." Then after another toddy or maybe even two, she said again, "It's really, really great to meet you, Bob." This went on for quite a while.

The next day, Claudette and I drove home to Birmingham. Just after we walked into the house, a Western Union telegram arrived (no e-mail or text messages in those days!). The message read, "It was a pleasure meeting you as well, Claudette. —Bob Costas."

What a classy move. The man just has a way with words!

Back when Bob and I were still cutting our teeth as broadcasters in the Eastern Hockey League, there was a player named Bill Goldthorpe, who was the model for the Ogie Ogilthorpe character in the movie *Slap Shot*. Goldthorpe was a big white guy who wore his hair in an unkempt Afro, as we called it back then. He was an absolute nut. If he wasn't certifiably insane, then he was waiting for the certificate to arrive any day. He would fight anybody, anytime, anywhere, for any reason.

He played for Syracuse, and in Bob's exact words, "Goldthorpe was not a learned man." Apparently, one day the Blazers were making a road trip, and Bob was sitting just in front of Goldthorpe. Bob was reading a magazine, minding his own business, and Goldthorpe was sleeping. Well, suddenly, Goldthorpe woke up, grabbed the magazine out of Bob's hands, looked at it, and tore it to shreds for no apparent reason. Without missing a beat, Bob leaned over and said to Goldthorpe, "Goldie, if you need to learn to read, just ask me, and I will be glad to tutor you."

To get a clear picture of what life was like as part of the Ducks organization, just think of the movie *Slap Shot*. In fact, several teams and events in the Eastern Hockey League actually inspired the 1977 Paul Newman film, which has remained a cult favorite. Hockey people, including myself, can quote the dialogue verbatim. It's easy for me to remember those classic lines because I was on those buses and in those arenas and watching those players—I lived *Slap Shot*!

The movie's fictitious team, the Charlestown Chiefs, was based on the Johnstown Jets, a real-life Eastern Hockey League team located in Johnstown, Pennsylvania. The movie's Hanson brothers were based on the real-life Carlson brothers—Steve, Jeff, and Jack—who played for the Jets. In the movie, Jeff and Steve Carlson played Jeff and Steve Hanson, while the part of their brother Jack was played by their teammate, David Hanson (hence the name, the Hanson brothers). Since Jack was on the road after having been called up to the Edmonton Oilers to play in the World Hockey Association play-offs, he missed the filming. I wonder if Jack regretted choosing the play-offs over the movie?

Paul Newman's character, player-coach Reggie Dunlop, is widely believed to have been based, at least in part, on the legendary Eastern Hockey League player (and later player-coach) John Brophy, whom I came to know extremely well.

Brophy, who was born in Halifax, Nova Scotia, was absolutely wild in his younger days. During his eighteen seasons in the Eastern Hockey League, he racked up nearly four thousand career penalty minutes, making him the league's most penalized player. Although he was play-ing for the Jersey Devils the year I joined the Ducks, he is more identi-fied with the Long Island franchise, which over the years traded him six times and acquired him back seven times. Brophy was often quoted as saying, "Once you're a Duck, you're a Duck for the rest of your life."

I'm not sure if Brophy was the inspiration for the Newman charac-ter in *Slap Shot*, but I do know that those who knew him took issue with part of the movie. In one scene, a character named "Brophy" is checked against the boards and someone says, "Brophy just pissed himself." They got that backward. If anybody was going to be inflict-ing pain, it was going to be Brophy. I personally witnessed his brand of tough, old-time hockey in action many times.

In the course of the season, the Ducks used to travel to Cherry Hill, New Jersey, to play the Jersey Devils, which were the Philadelphia Flyers' farm team, no relation to the current New Jersey Devils NHL franchise. In those days, the Devils played in the old Cherry Hill Arena, which was not exactly state-of-the-art. The arena was so old that it didn't even have glass around the boards; it had chicken wire. Something had to keep the puck in play!

For the most part, the chicken wire prevented the puck from sail-ing into the stands, but more often than not, the irregular surface would send the puck ricocheting in all directions.

Since this was the Devils' home arena, they learned the nuances of the chicken wire and often used it to their advantage. It was like play-ing basketball in an arena where you know the location of all the dead spots on the court. The Devils had one play where they would shoot the puck from the blue line directly into a certain section of the chicken wire, whereby it would bounce off and land directly in front of one of their guys standing in front of the opposing goal, waiting to knock it in right past the unsuspecting goaltender. Call it home-ice advantage.

The chicken wire created another interesting dynamic in Cherry

Hill (and other similar venues) due to the fact that the only thing standing between the rowdy players and the rowdy fans of the Eastern Hockey League (see *Slap Shot*) was wire with holes in it. Unfortunately, sometimes fans felt compelled to throw things at the players, and one night a guy in the corner of the stands spit on John Brophy.

Later in the game, Brophy skated to the same corner to retrieve the puck. He stopped, eyeballed the spitter, turned, and shoved the butt end of his stick through one of the holes in the chicken wire and knocked the guy's teeth out. There were ivories flying everywhere! Everyone was stunned. I was doing the play-by-play, so I know I said something. What it was, I don't remember. But I do remember what Brophy said: "Now spit, mother—!"

That's the way minor-league hockey was played in those days. These guys used to fight all the time. The Devils did, because the Philadelphia Flyers were a brawling hockey club, and a lot of the players thought the only way to get called up was to fight. It was the same way in Johnstown and other places too. You'd play for forty-five seconds and fight for forty-five minutes.

Probably the scrappiest Ducks game ever—fans still talk about it— was the legendary Midnight Game, which took place prior to my arrival with the team. The week before the game, the Ducks had traveled for four days in a raging snowstorm to play in Johnstown. They played, then traveled back to Long Island through another snowstorm for a home game against the New Haven Blades. The Ducks arrived at midnight, four hours late. The Blades, thinking the game was off, had gone down the street to watch a movie. But when the Ducks arrived, the fans, who were still gathered and enjoying plenty of beer at the concession stands, greeted them wildly. So the Blades were called back. The Ducks threw on their unwashed uniforms from their previous game and went straight from the bus to the ice. The puck was dropped, and a huge brawl ensued.

No one was sure if it was the stench of the uniforms or the players' pent-up frustration or the beer or the late hour or the cold or a toxic combination of all of the above, but the players pretty much punched their way through all three periods.

Certainly, the Eastern Hockey League wasn't all about fights. There was great action on the ice, and fans always had a nice view, since there really wasn't a bad seat in any of the small, band-box arenas. You were close to the players, and, more often than not, they were accessible. Kids could come down and get autographs from players during the warm-ups and certainly before and after the games.

Players were struggling, working-class guys you could relate to. They were kids from Swift Current and Moose Jaw, Saskatchewan, and Red Deer, Alberta. They had other jobs in the off-season. They slept on cots in the arena during tryouts. No wonder they played so brutally hard.

Sure, the fans were probably rowdier than in some other sports. But they weren't all like the grandma who hit a referee over the head with a broomstick. I mean, I married a woman I met at a minor-league hockey game! How I'd really describe these fans was loyal. Enthusiastic. These fans lived and died with their local teams. Or maybe they were just cold.

Any way you looked at it, the league was absolutely full of great stories, like the time a game was delayed because they couldn't find any pucks. (Someone found them stashed in an ice-cream freezer. Game on!) Or the time the Ducks borrowed the new, bright lights installed by their co-tenants, the ABA's New York Nets, only to find out that the heat from the lights melted the ice. Or the time the Zamboni driver, Henry James, crashed through the boards while waving to the fans. And of course the time a Ducks fan presented a Dixie Flyers player with a live chicken to retaliate for the insult hurled by his coach. (You don't call a Duck a chicken.)

A big part of the minor-league-hockey story is the buildings. At the Utica Memorial Auditorium in upstate New York, the owners didn't want to spend the money to paint the ice white. So, at the beginning of the game, the ice would appear the color of the asphalt floor underneath, whatever it was, either brownish or grayish. Then, as the game progressed, the snow that was generated by the skates would turn the ice white and—voilà—you had the effect of white ice. The only trouble was the players and the broadcasters could barely see the puck.

In New Haven there was no digital scoreboard. Instead, there was this panel with all these clock dials on it, like the scoreboard at the old Chicago Stadium, where the Blackhawks played. That thing had more hands than a massage parlor. I could never read it, so I'd just muddle through by making my best guess and never saying the exact time. "Folks, there's just over seven minutes left in the period . . ."

Even in the Central Hockey League, where I later worked, you deserved battle pay for even walking into some of the buildings. The Dallas Blackhawks, the Chicago Blackhawks' farm team, played in the arena immediately next door to the Cotton Bowl stadium. The press box was actually located directly behind the goal area. First of all, this was a terrible vantage point from which to see the action on the other end of the ice. Even worse was the fact that every time a player got ready to let one rip from the blue line, we literally had to dive for cover!

In the EHL the "arenas" were barns, really. Some were actually built incorrectly, with slanted walls and floors. These places had no amenities. The scoreboards had more lights out than lights on. The bathrooms were dirty. The concession stands turned out this gruel they tried to pass off as edible. And the broadcast booths, if you could call them that, were often places to test your bravery.

In Long Island the booth was off to the side but not behind glass. Although it never happened while I was there, a puck easily could have whizzed by and taken one of us out. In Cherry Hill they had a booth that was no more than a chicken coop hanging from the roof. It was attached at a bad angle, so you had to sit on a slant. Even then, I was not a small man, and I was always concerned that my *avoirdupois* might help bring the thing down out of the rafters. When I was up there, I just tried to hold really still. Which was sometimes hard, because we were shivering. I mean, you could see your breath when you spoke. Without exception, these buildings were really, really cold.

Once, at a Ducks game, fans in the stands actually started a bonfire to warm themselves. Hockey fans were adaptable. They knew what to expect. They lived in hockey communities, so they'd come to games all bundled up in their hats, gloves, and ski jackets. Broadcasters wore them too! I always wore three layers of clothing and never took my headphones off, since they served as a really good pair of earmuffs. Whatever worked.

There was an arena in Clinton, New York, that had virtually no exhaust system. When the Zamboni came out to resurface the ice, they had to throw open every door and window—literally every one—so the exhaust would have a place to go. Open the doors and windows for twenty minutes in Clinton, New York, in the dead of winter, where it's six degrees outside (i.e., a warm snap), and you'll feel what it's like to be cold. And there was hardly any heat in the building in the first place.

Cold was just part of the whole experience. To be sure, regardless of the temperature, on a Friday night when the Clinton Comets were playing at home, the hockey game was the place to be. You had to love it.

SIX

Twelve Years on a Bus

PEOPLE THINK I'M EXAGGERATING WHEN I SAY THAT I SPENT twelve years of my life on a bus. I really did! It wasn't as if I was on a submarine and couldn't get off. We did manage to step on terra firma from time to time. But basically, I spent more than a decade bumping along inside an old tin can that we affectionately called the Iron Lung.

For a brief time during my tenure as a minor-league-hockey announcer, we traveled by plane. It was an old DC-3 Gooney Bird, one of those World War II–era prop planes named after a Pacific island bird that is said to be clumsy on the ground and graceful in the air. Not sure about the graceful-in-the-air part. One thing I do know, that thing was slow. But none of us should have complained, because the budget for plane travel soon dried up, and it was back to the bus.

From 1971 to 1973 I traveled by bus with the Long Island Ducks, between New York and Massachusetts, Rhode Island, North Carolina, Florida and back again. In 1973 the team folded when the NHL expansion brought the New York Islanders to Long Island. This got me back on the bus for another season with the newly formed Long Island Cougars of the North American Hockey League (the farm team for the Chicago Cougars of the World Hockey Association). We bumped up the road to upstate New York, western Pennsylvania, Maine, and a few places in between. That'll raise the welts on your behind!

Then, in 1974 when I was hired to do the play-by-play for the Roanoke Valley Rebels of the Southern Hockey League, I rode the bus with the team throughout the South for a year. The next season, when the Rebels folded, I followed the coach, John Brophy, over to the Tidewater region of Virginia and became the play-by-play man for the Southern Hockey League team in Hampton. Once again I was back on the bus this time for the Hampton Gulls.

The buses we rode were not glamorous. They were not the customized sleeper buses of today, with all the electronics, flat-screen TVs, refrigerators, and other amenities. These were straight-ahead buses with straight-up seats. The team got them right off the rack. We rode the old, retired Greyhound that just a few days prior was ferrying people from New York to Pittsburgh.

Then there were the smells. Imagine twenty-three guys on a ten-hour bus ride. It was bad enough when the bathroom backed up and sewage would flow down the aisle. But there's just something about a large group of men confined together when no women are present. It's not pretty.

The hotels we stayed in were equally unglamorous. (Is there such a thing as a no-star hotel?) But these roadside dumps beat the bus. You know it's bad when you actually look forward to checking into a flea-bag motel!

On some of the buses there actually were a couple of sleeping bunks, which were always claimed by players (certainly not broadcasters) according to seniority. During one road trip from Long Island to Syracuse, I was so sick that I could barely sit up straight, so the guys let me sleep in a bunk for the duration of the five-hour drive. Otherwise, if you wanted to sleep, you had to attempt to do so sitting up or crouched down slightly in your seat with your head cocked to one side. I'm not built for bus travel, so sleeping was a particular challenge.

Another bus memory was on the Hampton Gulls' team bus, traveling from Virginia to New York. At one point while we were chugging up the road, I stretched out my legs across the aisle and managed to fall asleep. One of my feet somehow ended up on the headrest of John Brophy's seat. We were going up I-95 through Baltimore when "Broph" decided to grab my foot and bite it. Hard.

Of course I was jolted awake. "What the . . . ?"

He said, "Hey, see that building over there? That's the Bromo-Seltzer building. I climbed that building once."

I was stunned.

"OK," he said. "You can go back to sleep now."

Go back to sleep? Who can go back to sleep with a throbbing foot, not to mention the French Foreign Legion marching through your mouth? Defeated, I looked out the window at the Bromo-Seltzer building, which back in the 1920s was the tallest building in Baltimore, famous for its 51-foot-tall, rotating, blue Bromo-Seltzer bottle. I tried to picture Brophy climbing the 288-foot tower, which didn't take much imagination at all. Then I checked my foot for teeth marks.

I guess I asked for it, dangling my stocking feet in front of the man who accumulated more penalty minutes than any other player in the history of the Eastern Hockey League. You'd think he'd have mellowed since becoming a coach. And, in fact, compared to his playing days, which were peppered with stick fights, bench-clearing brawls, and a suspension for knocking down a referee, he had. (Although he was an intense coach). Players tell stories of him ripping his jacket to shreds in the locker room or throwing his wristwatch against the wall when his team trailed between periods. Anyway, I never had to meet him on the ice, and I consider myself lucky to count him among my dearest friends. I learned so much about hockey and about life from this man. He wasn't a surrogate father—he wasn't a father figure at all—but he had experience, and he knew his stuff.

Brophy was the definition of an old-time, rough, aggressive hockey player (see penalty factoid and movie *Slap Shot*). At age forty he retired as a player and became a coach for the Long Island Cougars. (Technically this wasn't his first year as a coach; he was briefly player-coach for the same club when they were known as the Long Island Ducks). Next, he headed south to coach the Roanoke Valley Rebels. When the Rebels folded, he went on to coach the Hampton Gulls for four seasons. When that team disbanded, he joined the Birmingham Bulls of the World Hockey Association as assistant to head coach Glen Sonmor. In 1978 Sonmor joined the Minnesota North Stars, and Brophy assumed the position of head coach and was later named the WHA's coach of the year.

In 1981 Brophy went home to Canada to coach the Nova Scotia Voyageurs, the Montreal Canadiens' AHL affiliate. After three seasons there, he joined the Toronto Maple Leafs as an assistant coach, then became head coach of their AHL affiliate, the St. Catharines Saints. Then, Brophy got his big break when he won the job as the NHL's Toronto Maple Leafs' head coach for the 1986–87 season.

Claudette and I traveled to Toronto to watch his very first game. Afterward, we met for dinner at a restaurant on Young Street. When Brophy walked in, everybody recognized him—it was impossible to miss that shock of white hair—and stood up to give him a standing ovation! It was the coolest thing.

Unfortunately, Brophy was fired after two and a half seasons in Toronto but immediately returned to coaching in the minor leagues, where he spent the remainder of his coaching days before retiring in

2008 at age seventy-five. In fact, he had retired a bit earlier, but the Richmond Renegades, a new team in the Southern Professional Hockey League, lured him out of retirement in 2006, saying there was no one more knowledgeable about hockey than Brophy.

I went to see Brophy when the Renegades came to play the Huntsville Havoc that year. By the time the game was over, four of his players had been thrown out. It was like a flashback to our old EHL days. I couldn't help thinking I had seen this script before!

What I remember most about those days—those years—on the buses is talking with Brophy. He and I used to talk for miles and miles. And when we weren't talking, he'd toss me his checkbook and a pile of his mail that he'd picked up during our brief stop at home and say, "Could you take care of these for me?"

Obediently I'd go through his letters and pay his bills. I didn't mind. It was something to do on the bus during those interminably long rides. Then, when we got to an arena, we'd walk the hallways together on a day off or after the morning skate. At the Cambria County War Memorial in Johnstown, the walls were covered with pictures, and we'd walk along while he pointed to each one and told me a story about this player or that coach. Certainly, he was one of the most knowledgeable people who had never been to class. I appreciated the education.

I didn't spend my entire twelve years on the bus with hockey players; I spent part of the time with baseball players too. From 1979 to 1983 I did the play-by-play for the Southern League's Birmingham Barons, which was the Double-A affiliate of the Detroit Tigers at the time. Since 1986 the club has been affiliated with the Chicago White Sox, which brought them a slew of media attention back in 1994, when Michael Jordan retired briefly from basketball and played for them for a year.

The Barons are a storied club, dating back to the 1880s when they were known as the Birmingham Coal Barons. For much of their existence and all of the time I was with them, the Barons played at Birmingham's Rickwood Field, the oldest professional ballpark in the country. It's a great throwback facility, complete with antique lamps and old-time billboards in the outfield. Although the team now plays at Regions Park in Hoover, Alabama, they still return to Rickwood once each season for the annual Rickwood Classic, where teams compete in vintage uniforms, and if you squint, you swear you're looking at an old film from the 1930s.

I love the minor leagues. When you mention the minors, people often think of the laid-back atmosphere and the folksy promotions. The Barons used to bring in Max Patkin, the clown prince of baseball, or the former Cleveland Indians pitcher Bob Feller, who would throw batting-practice-type pitches to fans. And, of course, Ted Giannoulas, a guy better known as the San Diego Chicken, would drop by from time to time. There were fireworks and the twenty-five-cent hot dog nights. All that was fine. But I really liked the sporting event. I went for the game.

The Tigers had a really good minor-league organization and fielded some great Double-A teams in those years. And attendance was good. In 1981 the Barons boasted their largest opening-night crowd (9,185) in more than thirty years when they beat Jacksonville (6-5) to open the season. In 1983 the Barons won the Southern League title, again, besting Jacksonville for the honor. During those years, fans were cheering the likes of MLB-bound players such as Howard Johnson, Bobby Melvin, Dwight Lowry, and Bruce Fields, to name a few.

I'd always go down to Lakeland, Florida, every March to broadcast the last few spring-training games back to the folks in Birmingham. The owners hoped this would spike ticket sales; in fact, the entire broadcast was like a two-and-a-half-hour commercial, "Get ready . . .

the Barons are coming; here's your starters for this year; watch out for Joe Shmoe!"

In the minors the players are so approachable. Especially during spring training. I loved hanging around the batting cages and talking to the players and being so close to the action. And even though your head didn't exactly swell when you were covering an exhibition game between the Birmingham Barons and the Chattanooga Lookouts, it was still, for me, the big leagues. Plus, there were palm trees swaying behind the outfield fence, and it was seventy degrees and sunny. If only you didn't have to get back on that bus . . .

As great as it was working in the minors, it could be dangerous for broadcasters. In minor-league ballparks the press box is often located directly over or behind the home plate area. Many times foul balls would be hit right back into the booth. There were nights when I did nothing but dodge foul balls. I couldn't even begin to count how many balls I have at the house. For some strange reason, I kept them all. A souvenir of my night's work, I suppose!

Since the ball was often deflected your way, it was important to be able to see it. But a lot of the fields had terrible lights, making it a challenge to keep track of that little, white ball.

The other thing was, the season was really long. The Barons played just a month less than guys in the majors did. There were virtually no days off. There were days in August when I'd be walking up to the booth, just praying for a rain cloud. I just wanted a day off, and there weren't any. On the plus side, when we traveled to a town, since the team usually played several games in a row, we'd stay in one place for a few days. On the minus side, we weren't staying in the Hyatt. In fact, we couldn't even see the Hyatt from most of the places we stayed.

I had to love what I was doing, because it could get tedious: Go to the game. Go to the Waffle House and talk the waitress into putting in your order for a double patty melt plate even though the kitchen just closed. Go back to your room and, in my case, stay up until two in the morning doing stats. (Broadcasters were also in charge of the team stats, and we did them by hand. Every day. Without computers.) Get up in the morning, read the paper, make some more notes, go back to the ballpark, and do it all again.

What made it easier for me was the fact that the Barons were always competitive. They won the championship one year, got to the finals another year. So I was not with a franchise that was playing out the string in May, where you had to go to the ballpark and you're thirty-seven games out of first place, ready to commit *hara-kiri*. (Or should I say, Harry Caray?)

I truly do not mean to complain. I have awesome memories of these days, and I was fully aware that I was putting in my time to get to the next level. You have to earn your chops. Besides, I think minor-league broadcasters had it easy compared to the umpires.

Minor-league umpires make very little money. These guys would bunk three to a room in a dumpy motel to keep costs low. And speaking of twelve years on a rickety bus? Umpires have to drive themselves. At least I didn't have to worry about falling asleep at the wheel just shy of Americus, Georgia. But we were all in this together. Everybody wanted to make it to the bigs. One guy who did was longtime MLB ump Jerry Layne, a dear friend.

I first met Jerry nearly thirty years ago. The Barons were playing the Savannah Braves (the Double-A affiliate of the Atlanta Braves) in Savannah, Georgia. The venue, Grayson Stadium, was a flea-infested converted football stadium, complete with football-style bleachers along the outfield and a baseball diamond crammed in the middle. The Braves didn't draw many fans—there were maybe four hundred people in attendance this particular night. But the stadium did draw no-see-ums, those little invisible sand fleas that nip at your ankles! There were plenty of those.

The radio booth at Grayson Stadium was directly over home plate. I had to sit flush against the table, lean way over, and look down to see home plate. As a result, especially since I have a loud voice and there was a bit of an echo due to the small crowd, nobody in the stadium missed a thing I said. Especially the guys at home plate—the batter, the catcher, and the home plate umpire, which that night was Jerry Layne.

Pitching for the Barons that evening was a kid named Bryan Kelly, a prospect from the University of Alabama. He was a fireballing thrower; he must have thrown ninety-nine miles per hour on every pitch, but during that game, his accuracy was nowhere to be found.

Over the course of the evening, Kelly walked at least fifteen guys, and for whatever reason, the manager didn't pull him. He was just going to let Kelly throw until he got his act together. It got so bad it was almost funny. I mean, these pitches were nowhere near the strike zone.

During the broadcast I made it a point to say that the ump was not squeezing the strike zone. What he was doing, though, was cleaning home plate. Over and over. He kept coming out from behind the plate, with his whisk broom in hand, and dusting it off. I had never seen home plate so clean. What else were you going to do? Every time he'd knock the dust off the plate, he'd look up at the radio booth and roll his eyes, with this hilarious look on his face. That was the day our friendship began.

Not long ago, I was speaking at a University of Alabama alumni chapter meeting in Orlando. Prior to the meeting, a guy walked up to me and said, "I bet you don't remember me." The face looked familiar, but I couldn't place him. Well, it was Bryan Kelly, now an Orlando businessman who just happened to be the pitcher who threw those umpteen walks all those years ago. We laughed about it, and since

Kelly was such a good sport, I got my cell phone and dialed Jerry. He was in Cincinnati, in the umpire's dressing room. I said, "Jerry, I'd never bother you at work, but you've got to say hello to somebody." He definitely remembered Kelly, and they immediately launched into a discussion of that long, long night.

It's easy to keep track of Jerry just by watching baseball on TV. Not long ago, I was watching a Yankees game where Jerry was the home plate ump. At one point, I saw Jerry; Yankees manager Joe Torre; the catcher, Jorge Posada; and the pitcher, all standing around laughing. The next day I called Jerry to ask him what was so funny.

Evidently, it all went back to an incident that took place during a World Series game many years prior. In the middle of an inning, the Dodgers' pitcher was struggling, so the manager, Tommy Lasorda, came out to the mound to discuss a pitching change with his pitcher and catcher. The home plate umpire, John McSherry, stood nearby. First Lasorda asked the pitcher, "How do you feel?" The pitcher said, "I feel pretty good." Then Lasorda looked to the catcher and asked, "Does he still have his stuff?" The catcher replied, "Yeah, I think so." Then Lasorda turned toward McSherry and said, "Mac, what do you think?" McSherry answered, "If I were you, I'd take him out. I think he's lost something." Well, they all cracked up.

As it turned out, McSherry was miked during that game, not for the live broadcast but for World Series highlights to be used at a later time. So MLB officials heard McSherry's joke. And they fined him. They didn't want there to be the appearance of an umpire making any sort of strategic decision for a team.

So, back to Jerry on TV.

The Yankees were playing. The pitcher was struggling, and manager Joe Torre walked out to the mound to discuss a pitching change with his pitcher and catcher. The home plate umpire, Jerry, stood nearby. Torre asked his pitcher how he felt. "OK, Skip . . ." He asked the catcher to weigh in. "He's still got it." Then he looked at Jerry. All the guys on the field knew the McSherry story, so when Jerry answered, "I don't make as much money as McSherry. Sorry. You're on your own," they all had a belly laugh.

Jerry paid his dues in the minor leagues, and not only is he now acknowledged as one of the best umpires in baseball, but he's also on ESPN, laughing with Joe Torre.

Back in the minors, play-by-play guys often pulled double or triple duty. On top of calling the games, we also played the role of part-time public relations guy and team statistician. With the Barons I'd start keeping stats from the beginning of the season. I'd literally get a blank piece of paper and, after the first game, I'd fill in all the boxes. Then I'd update the page after the second game, the third game, the twenty-ninth game, all the way to game 147. I did this every day whether we were on the road or at home.

Not only did I do the cumulative team stats, but I'd also keep stats for every individual player so I could access information quickly. If a guy hit a triple, I could see on the big sheet that it was his fourth triple of the year; and while I was talking, I could quickly go to his personal page and see that he hadn't hit a triple since May 7, when the Barons were at home. Does that matter to the outside world? Probably not. Does that make you a better broadcaster? I think so.

It was my responsibility to keep the stats not just for the broadcast but for the team's purposes as well. Sometimes the manager would ask, "How's Johnson doing with RBIs? What are the numbers?" So I'd keep track of what the team was doing by watching, but I also had to do my research. In those days there were no Internet sites to find information. There was no Elias Sports Bureau feeding me facts. When I needed to do research, I either made phone calls or looked things up in books, newspapers, or magazines. Or, if I was lucky, the team had a guy like Bill Shipp.

Bill was a guy who never missed a Barons game. He'd been around forever, with the Barons and the Birmingham A's, the Oakland A's farm team. He may not have always had the exact statistic you wanted, but I would call him on occasion and say, "Bill, did you ever hear of a pitcher striking out the same guy twelve times in a row?" And he would know. Or you'd find somebody else who knew his stuff. Once we were in Columbus, Georgia, and somebody hit a mammoth home run. During the commercial break, I ran over to the writers' section of the press box and asked, "Anybody ever seen a home run bigger than that in this park?" Somebody answered, "Yeah, Harmon Killebrew hit a home run that landed over in that lake back in 1962." Then I ran back to the booth and went on the air and started telling the story about Killebrew, making sure to stretch it out for a while. "Folks, you remember Harmon Killebrew? . . . Here's the one-one to Johnson . . . well, back in 1962, he was having quite a year . . . here's the two-two . . . I remember back when Killebrew was playing for the Twins. It must have been a home run like this one."

That's how we did it back then. You gathered the facts and turned it into a story. Preferably a long one.

Minor-league announcers are a one-man band. You do the stats, the engineering, and all parts of the broadcast. You don't have a color analyst. It's you and only you. But if you're prepared—and you had better be prepared to talk for a full nine innings—it can be lot of fun. What I like about baseball, from a broadcaster's point of view, is the pace. Unlike other sports, such as hockey or racing, which move far more quickly, baseball is slower paced, so you can tell stories and let your personality come out. You can take a story that normally takes thirty seconds and stretch it out for an entire inning. In fact, it behooves you to do that. An on-air guy doesn't want to tell everything he knows about a batter during the guy's first at-bat. Then what do you do for the other eight innings?

In football it's different. You have all this research, and if you get a chance to talk about a guy, you usually throw in as many facts as you can. You may never see that player again or he may not make another great play, so if he's the man of the moment, use your factoids. But in baseball you take it slow.

Since the season was so long and the bus rides seemed even longer, everyone would try to find things to occupy themselves as we put miles between those minor-league towns. I would try to do my stats on the bus, but sometimes that proved challenging, since there was so much noise—singing, laughing, snoring, farting! Or, when I tried to type my stats on my trusty portable Olivetti typewriter (I would actually haul that thing with me), sometimes I'd quit because I was disturbing the players. In those days we didn't have iPods or DVD players to drown out the noise. So unless you wanted to stuff toilet tissue in your ears, you simply put up with it.

Some guys passed the time by reading. One guy who always read on the bus was Eddie Brinkman, the former Detroit Tigers shortstop who managed the Barons in 1982. Brinkman, who had a great fifteen-year career in the majors, was known as a "good field, no hit" player. He was one of the worst hitters in baseball but made a great living with his glove. As it turned out, in Birmingham he was a fantastic hitting instructor.

At the start of spring training, Brinkman went out and bought the biggest, fattest mystery novel he could find. A paperback book with some seven hundred pages that would occupy his time on the bus. He only read it on the road and would try to time it so he finished the book and found out whodunit right at the end of the season. That was his ritual.

During one of our first road trips, when Brink wasn't looking, I took his book and ripped out the last thirty pages. Normally I would hate to ruin a book, but this was a used, tattered paperback and, well, I was on a mission. I didn't destroy them; rather, I stowed the thirty pages in my attaché case and left them there. I carried the pages around with me all season, but after a month or so, I forgot about them.

Then came September. We were busing to Florida for a series against the Jacksonville Suns. Brinkman was sitting behind the bus driver. I was in the front seat across from him, half asleep, and Bob Melvin, our catcher who went on to a great major-league career and was the manager of the Arizona Diamondbacks for a few years, was sitting in the second row behind the driver, right behind Brink, also dozing.

All of a sudden Brink started yelling. Why? He was out of pages, but the murderer hadn't yet been revealed. Well, he strung together a bunch of expletives; there were more hyphens in that curse than Carter had liver pills. He woke up Melvin and said, "You slimy, greasy SOB!" Of course, Melvin, who had—and still has—this young, angelic face, had no idea what he was talking about. Brink was shaking down everyone, even a couple of the non–English-speaking guys, who only partly understood what he was saying. He was spitting nails! He accused everyone!

The only person he didn't accuse was the mild-mannered broadcaster sitting across the aisle from him. I had forgotten that I had those pages until that very moment. And I didn't say a word.

The Barons went on to the play-offs, then returned to Birmingham. As we pulled up to Rickwood Field and concluded our final trip, I reached into my attaché case and pulled out the pages. As we were getting off the bus, I handed them to Brink. "I believe these are yours."

He just stared at me. He didn't know whether to laugh or cry. Or curse!

After he left Birmingham, Brinkman moved to Chicago and

finished his career as a scout and an infield coach for the White Sox. Sadly, he passed away in 2008. But I'm glad to say I went to see him in Chicago once. Claudette and I went to a White Sox game, and afterward Brink took me down to the clubhouse. As we were walking out, he smiled with that great, rubbery face of his and said, "I've not forgotten about the book. Paybacks are hell."

That would be the last time I saw Brink.

SEVEN

The Puck Stops Here

NO BROADCASTER LIKES TO MAKE A MISTAKE ON THE AIR. BUT we're human. Eventually, even the best of the best will have a slip of the tongue. When it comes to broadcasting hockey, there is one particular land mine we all must navigate: the word *puck*.

It's not a difficult word. It's a one-syllable, punchy noun. But it's a word we use often, sometimes a couple dozen times per game. And it can trip you up.

One night back in the late '70s, I was doing the play-by-play for a World Hockey Association game in Cincinnati. The Birmingham Bulls were playing the Cincinnati Stingers, who had a great player, an American named Robbie Ftorek (pronounced *fi-tor-eck*). This guy went on to play in the NHL and coached for the New York Rangers; he's a Hall of Famer. Anybody who knows hockey knows Robbie Ftorek.

During the game Ftorek was skating down the ice, and instead of saying, "Here comes Ftorek with the puck," I said, "Here comes *Pitorek* with the . . ."

Yes, I swapped the first letter of each word. Could have happened to anyone, but this was a live broadcast. Over the years I've heard stories of many play-by-play guys experiencing similar, equally horrifying moments. ESPN's Jon Miller admits that during the first game he called for the NHL's California Golden Seals way back when, he got tongue-tied while trying to say, "The puck fell." Instead he said . . . well, you know what he said. According to Miller, ever after he has advised aspiring hockey announcers to refer to the puck as "it."

After my misspeak, though I was horrified, I did what most broadcasters do in this situation—absolutely nothing.

Over the years I've learned that it is a wise approach to not call too much attention to a flub, unless, of course, it's a serious, factual flub. But after a mere misstep, it's best to just move on. My reasoning has always been that even though people are listening to you, they aren't necessarily hanging on your every syllable. Imagine a conversation somewhere out there in the listening audience: "Harry, did I just hear what I think I heard?" and Harry says, "What? He didn't say that. Are you crazy?"

If you stop, you bring attention to the mistake. In certain situations you might make a small, humorous aside, but otherwise, move on. In hockey you have no choice, because the game moves so incredibly fast, and you have to keep up with the pace. You also have to keep up with the names.

When I started doing hockey in the early '70s, there had yet to be the influx of the Russian, Czech, Swedish, and Ukrainian players we have today. We had names like Butch Morris and Larry Billows. Sure, we had a few Claude Chartres, but we also had plenty of Mike Smiths. These days, rosters are full of names like Branko Radivojevic and Jaroslav Halak. So you have to be prepared.

What I usually do is write down the names of the players phonetically. I do this for all sports, but it's especially important in hockey, where many of the names are tongue twisters. Of course, you get to know your own players when you're working for one team. The challenge is to learn the names of the opposing team. I'd always get together with the opponent's broadcaster before every game and make sure my pronunciations were correct.

When I was with the Hampton Gulls, we played an exhibition game against the Moscow Dynamo team, which consisted of all the biggest names from the former Soviet Union. Before the game, I contacted a Russian professor at a nearby university and had him teach me some Russian phrases. This was a big, big game. The place was sold out. I really wanted to do something different, so I learned how to go to commercial breaks in Russian. So, instead of saying, "You're listening to Hampton Gulls hockey," I would say, *"Bbi cnywaete k hockey Hampton Gulls."*

I realized that few if any of our listeners spoke Russian. But I wanted to go the extra mile. How many times do the Russians come to Hampton, Virginia, to play hockey?

Years later, an altogether different Russian all-star team came to the University of Alabama when I was doing the play-by-play for the basketball team. The SEC worked out a deal with an international sports federation where teams from the former Soviet Union, including teams from Belarus, Uzbekistan, Kazakhstan, Tajikistan, Stan Laurel—all these different Stans!—would come over to play preseason basketball against teams from the SEC.

Before the game, color analyst Tom Roberts and I sat down with the liaison from the Russian Sports Federation (I thought he was from the KGB) to review the pronunciations of the players' names. Many of the names were fairly long and seemed to have either all vowels or all consonants, never enough of each! Again, we wrote down the names phonetically, not that our broadcast was going to be heard in Moscow, but at the same time the players deserved to have their names pronounced correctly.

The Russians won the opening tip, and the ball went right to their guard, Number 5, a little guy named Lubomir Yourin (pronounced *Loo-bo-meer Your-in*).

Before I could catch myself, I said, "Here comes Yourin, dribbling down the court."

Of course, Tom and I, being the grown-up children we are, started laughing like hyenas. For the remainder of the game, our self-control would be tested sorely because the guy had a great game. "Here's Number 5 in the deep corner. He puts up the shot, nothing but net. Yourin is hot tonight!"

I guess it was a good thing it was a preseason game.

When the NHL expanded in 1972 and the New York Islanders began play, it spelled the end of the minor league hockey franchise in New York. Therefore, when I was offered the job as play-by-play announcer for the Roanoke Valley Rebels, I jumped on it. My friend John Brophy was the coach in Roanoke, and I knew a lot of the other people involved with the team. I was excited about the job. And even though I loved my hometown, I was ready to leave New York.

First of all, as an aspiring broadcaster, the Big Apple was a beyond-competitive market. Guys with names like Cosell and Albert and Wolff had things sewed up in the early '70s. I'm not trying to say I was in contention for their jobs (or would have ever been in contention), but a young guy had a better chance of climbing the broadcast ladder outside New York. Plus, I knew I wasn't ready for the big leagues. I needed more experience, so I went south.

Roanoke was a great town to work in. Not only was it the home of the famous Weenie Stand, the lunch spot that served the best chili dogs in history, but it was home to a brand-new arena, the Roanoke Civic Center, where the Rebels played. Virginia Tech was also close by, although they weren't the sports powerhouse they are today. Perhaps that's why the fans appreciated the hockey team—they were practically the only game in town.

Roanoke was also the place I proposed to my wife, Claudette. We met in New York at a hockey game—she was a big fan of the Long Island Ducks—and we dated for a few years. Then, when she came to visit me in Roanoke, I asked her to marry me. Her response? She promptly spit her chewing gum in my face.

Some guys would think that was a no, but I knew she was just surprised, even flabbergasted. When she collected herself and her gum, she said yes.

After the Rebels ceased operations, I was offered the job as play-by-play guy for the Hampton Gulls, so I moved to Newport News, Virginia, and my new bride joined me there. Claudette got a job managing an apartment complex, and she did it well. Part of the reason for this was that she made a habit of going right to the top.

Some of the apartments in her complex were occupied by players for the Peninsula Pilots, the Single-A farm club for the Philadelphia Phillies. One year, the Pilots won the Carolina League Championship, and after the play-offs were over, many of the players simply skipped town without paying their rent. Beyond that, some of the guys had thrown big parties in their apartments prior to leaving and left the place in shambles.

Even though it was after hours, Claudette was anxious to reach someone immediately to inform them about what all had transpired, so she called her contact with the Pilots, who actually worked out of the Phillies office in Philadelphia. Being as late as it was, the phone rang and rang and rang. Finally, a male voice answered the phone, "Phillies."

She explained who she was and what had happened. The gentleman couldn't have been nicer. He said, "We're embarrassed. We'll take care of this first thing in the morning. That's not how the Phillies or any of our minor leaguers do business."

Before hanging up, Claudette asked the guy for his name and extension so she could follow up the next day. Then, that night, she told me the story. I said, "Good for you." Then out of curiosity I asked, "Who did you speak to?"

She said, "Ruly Carpenter."

"Ruly Carpenter!"

"Yes," she said. "Why? Do you know him?"

I said, "Claudette, that's the owner of the Phillies!"

She just shrugged. I mean, it was as if she had called the Yankees and George Steinbrenner answered the phone. Carpenter must have been the only one in the office that evening and answered a phone that just wouldn't stop ringing! You better believe she collected the rent.

Although I saw the move from the Rebels to the Gulls as a step up of sorts, I was still a minor-league broadcaster, which meant that I was a one-man band. I not only called the games; I set up my own equipment, did the statistics, put out press releases, and also made travel arrangements for the team.

For the first year I was with the Hampton Gulls, and for two seasons prior to my arrival, the team competed in the Southern Hockey League, winning the 1976–77 regular-season championship. The following year the Southern Hockey League folded, and the Gulls took a step up when they were approved as an expansion franchise in the American Hockey League. Sadly, though, the team folded halfway through the following season due to the financial strain of competing in the higher league.

Since the Gulls were the farm team for the Birmingham Bulls, the World Hockey Association team that had relocated from Toronto, I

Resplendent in a "Leisure Suit" while broadcasting a mid-1970s hockey game in Greensboro, NC

knew some folks in Birmingham. When I became available, the owner, John Bassett, invited me to join the broadcast crew.

I moved to Birmingham. (Claudette joined me a few months later.) On my third day in town, I boarded the team plane for a flight to Edmonton for the start of a road trip through western Canada. (What, no bus?) We stayed in a hotel next to the coliseum. A nice one. With clean sheets and room service. This was a whole new world.

I loved the road trips. And I loved Birmingham, which became and remains my adopted home. My impressions of the place were wonderful. I was born and raised in New York City, and I'd had enough of the hassles. Even today when I go and visit, I'll hop in a cab at the airport to take me to midtown, and it doesn't take me ten minutes to remember why I left! I love to visit New York and other great cities from Denver to Quebec to Los Angeles, but I prefer a smaller town as my home.

We had some truly talented players in Birmingham, including young future NHL players Rick Vaive, Michel Goulet, Craig Hartsburg, and Rob Ramage, as well as exceptional veterans, such as Paul Henderson and Frank Mahovlich. The Bulls faced some great teams with many great players, including a certain seventeen-year-old named Wayne Gretzky, who was playing for the Indianapolis Racers. Everyone knew who Gretzky was; he was the talk of the hockey world. In fact, John Bassett had tried hard to recruit him for the Bulls. The first day Gretzky came to Birmingham, I made it a point to watch the pregame practice so I could see him in action. At one point, I went up to him to say hello. The guy who arguably became the greatest player to ever play the game was actually an incredibly shy young man at the time, so we didn't have much of a conversation. Then, as Gretzky skated away, I remember saying to myself, "Man, this guy's got bird legs. I don't know if he's going to make it in this business."

Across the street from the civic center where the Bulls played was this place called The Place Across the Street from the Civic Center. That was its name. Basically, it was a bar that served sandwiches, and all the Bulls players and players from the visiting team would go there after the games. I used to go there with friends, like Butch Owens, the guy who became my longtime spotter for Alabama football games, as well as NFL and arena football games. Since so many years have passed, I believe it would be OK to say that Butch used to buy beer for Gretzky, since he was not yet of legal drinking age.

Not long ago, I saw Gretzky at a Phoenix Coyotes game, where he was filling his current role of head coach, part-owner, and head of hockey operations for the team. I said hello to him and reminded him of our acquaintance in Birmingham all those years ago.

The first thing he said was, "Is that place across from the civic center still there?" Sadly, I had to tell him that the place is gone. I didn't mention my earlier thoughts about his bird legs.

The Bulls played some exceptionally exciting games. One that stands out is the night the lights went out in Springfield, Massachusetts. We were playing the New England Whalers, as they were called at the time, in their old fairgrounds-based building, the Eastern States Coliseum, known as the Big E. (The Whalers were temporarily relocated there when the roof of the Hartford Civic Center collapsed following a snowstorm.)

The Whalers had some powerhouse players, such as future Hall of Famers Gordie Howe and Gerry Cheevers. Howe, whom many people refer to as "Mr. Hockey," went on to be one of the greatest players in history and the only player to compete in the NHL in five different decades. Cheevers, an aggressive, driven goaltender, is often remembered for his wild-looking mask. (Every time a puck struck his mask, he marked the spot with a painted stitch.)

That night, however, Howe, Cheevers, and company were putting up a tough fight when the Bulls' Wayne Dillon, came in, skating left to right, coming down left wing. He wound up to take the shot—an incredible shot it was—and while the puck was in midflight, the arena suddenly went completely dark. The building blew a fuse! The fans let out a collective, "Whoaaa!" as the players dove to the ground because no one knew where the heck the puck was. Dillon's shots often left his stick at a hundred miles per hour! The goaltender was padded, of course, but in those days players didn't wear as much protection as they do today. (Incredibly, the NHL didn't require new players to wear helmets until 1979. Even then, old players could choose to wear them or not!)

The lights were completely out in the building, except for a few scattered areas, including the press box. We had power, but the ice and surrounding area was pitch-black. But we were able to stay on the air, and if I didn't know it already, this was a fantastic lesson regarding why a sportscaster should always overprepare for a game. I had a lot of time to fill (there was no way to know exactly how much), and back then, there was no studio to throw it back to!

The fans mostly just sat in their seats and stared at the dark ice or gingerly made their way to the concession stands. Some of the players skated around to keep loose or waited on the bench. As for me, I talked and talked. Then I grabbed whomever I could to interview—the late Jimmy Bryan, the Bulls' beat writer for the *Birmingham News*, or a team scout—then I talked some more. After nearly thirty minutes, the lights came back on, the game resumed, and my blood pressure returned to just above normal.

Every broadcaster who works for more than one team and covers more than one sport (and many of us do) eventually faces the challenge of trying to be in two places at once. Of course, for live events it's impossible; but sometimes, with a little creativity, you can find a solution.

One Friday I had an overlap on my schedule. The Bulls were playing at the arena in Birmingham the same evening that the state 6A high school football championships were to be played at Legion Field. I was supposed to cover both. Obviously, I was going to have to opt out of one of the events, until my buddy Butch Owens offered to help.

Since the radio broadcast of the hockey game was live, I had to be there. But since the football game was not due to air on cable TV until the following day, we could tape the game and fill in the play-by-play after the fact. So that's what we did.

I went to the hockey game, where it was business as usual. Butch went to the football game, and while the camera crew taped the game with natural sound, he got the rosters and took copious notes, recording every play as it happened. After the hockey game, we met at a studio, ordered a bunch of pizzas (this was going to take a while), and got to work putting together the telecast.

These days it's commonplace to tape an event and fill in the "voice-over" after the fact. I've since done it many times. But in those days, especially in a smaller market, this was a first. That night, we just had fun with it. The engineers rolled the videotape of the game and added the audio as I did the play-by-play. The funny thing was, my color man, Tandy Geralds, a well-known former high school coach in Alabama, couldn't be with us to voice the game, so I simply referenced him occasionally: "You know, Tandy, they run this particular play really, really well . . ." But since Tandy wasn't there, he didn't answer. And I think—I hope—no one noticed his silence.

Since I knew the outcome of the game, as well as every play that was run ahead of time, once or twice I just couldn't help utilizing this proverbial crystal ball. I'd look at Butch's chart and see that the next play was going to be a quarterback draw. Then, as the players lined up, I'd say, "This would be the perfect spot to run the quarterback draw. And, yup! There it is! They pick up eighteen yards."

Obviously, I had an edge in predicting the future that day. What amazes me is when this happens for real during an NFL or Alabama game. Often, I've heard Kenny Stabler or another color analyst say, "What I'd do right here is run the 64-toss power trap," and then he would go on to explain why. Then, son of a gun, if they don't run that exact play! Now, that's magic.

The Birmingham Bulls were a great organization. If the team had stayed together, I have no doubt they would eventually have won a Stanley Cup. People called them "the Baby Bulls" because they had some of the best young talent in the world.

When the WHA disbanded in 1979, the Bulls were faced with the choice of either joining the NHL or the lower-rung Central Hockey League (CHL).

The owner of the team, John Bassett, was a savvy Canadian businessman who realized that Birmingham was a nontraditional market. We had terrific fans, but there was a steep learning curve; the first year the fans were applauding icing! Bassett felt that attendance was not going to increase just because the Bulls would be facing NHL opponents. Since it didn't really matter to the fans if we were playing the Indianapolis Racers or the Montreal Canadiens, he couldn't justify the greater expense in terms of salaries, travel, and so forth that joining the NHL would require. Therefore the Bulls became part of the CHL.

As soon as the news broke that the Bulls would soon be playing in the CHL, coaches and scouts from other NHL teams began to flock to town to scout the Baby Bulls, hoping to secure some of these players for the upcoming dispersal draft.

As a result, every NHL team had someone, either their GM or their assistant GM, attending every Bulls game, both home and away. If we were in Quebec City, the scouts would be there. The next night, in Edmonton, again, the scouts would be there. This turned out to be a fortuitous thing for me. In fact, this is how I got the job as the television play-by-play announcer for the NHL's St. Louis Blues.

Emile Francis was a huge name in hockey. He had been the coach, president, and GM of the New York Rangers for years, and in 1979 he was the president and GM of the St. Louis Blues. He and his trusted assistant, Dennis Ball, came to every Bulls game to scout our magnificent talent. As luck would have it, their seats were often directly beside me in the press box, so they were within earshot doing the broadcast of the Bulls game. Evidently, they made a note of my work because before long I would be invited to audition for the Blues.

I had long dreamed of becoming a broadcaster in the NHL. But in my wildest imagination I never thought I'd get a stab at a job with the

Blues, because their longtime voice was the legendary Dan Kelly, a Hall of Famer and without a doubt the best hockey broadcaster in America. (He was one of the broadcasters I wrote a letter to when I was a kid!) Dan Kelly was to hockey what Mel Allen and Vin Scully were to baseball. Truly one of the best broadcasters anywhere.

In St. Louis they had been doing a simulcast, meaning the play-by-play guy, Dan Kelly, and his color analyst, Gus Kyle, did the radio broadcast for KMOX radio, and their audio was simultaneously picked up by the TV station, KDNL, Channel 30. Well, a simulcast is always tricky. It hardly ever serves the viewers or the listeners. These days, almost every team in every sport splits the broadcast. In other words, there is a separate program for radio and television.

In this scenario things got contentious between KMOX and KDNL. The radio station wouldn't allow the broadcasters to allude to what was being seen on TV. They couldn't mention replays or even promote upcoming shows. Even though the quality of the hockey coverage was excellent, KDNL got fed up with the restrictions and decided to do their own broadcast.

At that point Emile Francis recommended "this kid from Birmingham" to do the TV play-by-play.

I can just hear the executives at KDNL saying, "Birmingham?" But when Emile Francis made a recommendation, people listened. As a result, Jack Petrik, the GM at KDNL, asked me to fly to St. Louis for an audition.

They put me in the studio, flicked on a light, and had me stand there by myself. From the dark of the control room, they asked me questions such as, "What is your philosophy on broadcasting a hockey game?" and "What would you say if the other team is doing real well and the Blues weren't doing so well?"

Basically, I answered that I was going to play it straight. There wouldn't be any question that they were tuning in to a St. Louis Blues telecast, but at the same time, if the Blues were trailing 5-0, I couldn't say that the Blues were playing well.

Then they had me read some promotional stuff: "Don't forget, *Hogan's Heroes* is coming up right after the game, followed by *The Beverly Hillbillies* on KDNL, TV-30." That was it. No play-by-play! We were done.

After the interview I went home and waited. After a few days the curiosity was killing me, so I called Jack. He said, "Oh, yeah. You got the job. Didn't anybody tell you?"

I couldn't have been more thrilled. As a kid, I was a Rangers season-ticket holder who stared up at the press box and dreamed of someday being in front of the microphone. And now, I would be doing play-by-play in the NHL. I'd be working in all these magnificent buildings—Maple Leaf Gardens, Chicago Stadium, the Detroit Olympia—that I'd only read about or seen on television. I was walking on air.

I'd get my feet back on the proverbial ground soon enough, though. How does that saying go? Be careful what you wish for.

Since the Blues' home games weren't televised on KDNL, I only worked road games. Usually, I traveled by myself from Birmingham and met the team on the road. When I first started, I truly thought the two stations had simply decided to split the broadcast. But I soon learned that I was just a pawn in their political struggle.

The situation was awkward for everybody because I was an outsider coming in and replacing Dan Kelly, a beloved broadcaster who was the very best in the NHL. Understandably, a lot of people rallied around Dan.

There was a sportswriter, Bob Verdi, a world-renowned columnist for the *Chicago Tribune* and a good friend of Dan Kelly's, who absolutely tarred, feathered, and skewered me on the front page of the Sports section after the announcement was made that I would be taking the job. He never had the decency to call me directly; and before meeting me or even hearing me on the air, he basically disemboweled me in print.

Despite this less-than-warm welcome from the *Tribune*, most of the people involved with the team and the TV station were very cordial, especially Dan Kelly. Obviously, Dan was not thrilled by what had transpired. But he understood that I wasn't the one who convinced KDNL to split the broadcasts. Most important, he was a gentleman. The very definition of class. Once, during a trip to Chicago, Dan took me, along with a few others, out to a restaurant, and we ran into baseball broadcasters Harry Caray and Jack Brickhouse, whom Dan knew and introduced me to. Just one of many wonderful nights working for the Blues.

I vividly remember my first-ever NHL broadcast at the old McNichols Arena in Denver, where the Colorado Rockies hockey team played. I was equally excited walking into the Met Center in Bloomington, Minnesota, and the old Memorial Auditorium (the Aud) in Buffalo when we played the Sabres. And when I walked into Madison Square Garden for the first time that season? Unbelievable.

My first trip to New York as a Blues broadcaster was for a game against the Islanders at the Nassau Coliseum. We were due to play the Rangers two days later, but as luck would have it, the next day I got a call from the Atlanta Flames to fill in for their color man, Bernie "Boom Boom" Geoffrion, that night.

For my first trip back to the Garden as a real broadcaster, I was sitting next to the Flames' play-by-play guy, Jiggs McDonald. It wouldn't have mattered to me if I had been sitting next to the man on the moon! Then, the very next night, I was back in the press box for the Blues–Rangers game. I couldn't help but look over in the direction of my old seats in section 440, Row F, and take it all in. No one will ever take that moment away from me.

Other highlights of that year included working in the new Joe Louis Arena in Detroit the very first night it opened and working in the L.A. Forum. I'd never been to Los Angeles, so I was completely agog. The director was in my ear, saying, "All right, when the action stops, we're going to show you Jack Nicholson," or "After the next stoppage we'll show you Dyan Cannon."

This is to certify that ELI GOLD OF KDNL-TV 30 ST. LOUIS DID THE FIRST EVER HOCKEY TELECAST AND *was present at the opening hockey game in the*

Joe Louis Sports Arena

on this the twenty-seventh day of December nineteen hundred and seventy-nine

Detroit Red Wings vs. St. Louis Blues

Signed: *Coleman A. Young*   Signed: *Ted Lindsay*

Coleman A. Young, Mayor
City of Detroit

Ted Lindsay, General Manager
Detroit Hockey Club

The plaque I received for broadcasting the first ever hockey game at the Joe Louis Arena in Detroit

My memories of bus rides to Johnstown, Pennsylvania, were beginning to fade. But lest I get too comfortable, there was always Gus Kyle.

A former defenseman for the Rangers and Bruins, Gus Kyle was the color analyst at KMOX for sixteen years. From the beginning, Kyle did his darnedest to make things difficult for me. He would give me wrong information, such as telling me the bus was leaving at five when it was really leaving at four thirty. He'd constantly call my room in the middle of the night to wake me up. And once, at the Statler Hilton Hotel in Buffalo, he walked by my room and kicked the door in . . . literally. He kicked the door down!

Kyle was upset that Dan Kelly and he were no longer doing the telecasts. I understood that. But what I didn't understand was why, in contrast to the tremendously classy Dan Kelly, he blamed me for it.

The fact was, the whole experience was difficult for me. This was my first stab at TV, and I never made the adjustment as well as I should have. I ended up talking too much. Looking back, I think I was doing radio on television. It makes sense because all I had done up to that point was radio.

On TV, you're basically putting captions on pictures. On radio, you're drawing the entire word picture. Not to denigrate anybody who works on TV, but I've always found radio far more challenging. I love the challenge of describing the smells, the sights, the sounds, the color of the sky, the color of the uniforms, and the entire ambiance of the event. I like to be able to make that come alive through the speaker of a radio. Which is something you don't have to do on television. You shut up and let the picture talk.

Happily, I would get another chance to do TV and continue to do radio for many, many years.

EIGHT

Coming and Going and Talking About Sports

DURING THE 1979–80 HOCKEY SEASON, I DID THE PLAY-BY-PLAY for both the St. Louis Blues on TV and the Birmingham Bulls on radio. My number one priority was the Blues telecasts, but the schedule almost always worked out for me to do both because the Bulls and Blues often played on alternating days. At the time, I was also doing NASCAR races for the Motor Racing Network (MRN) and basketball games for the brand-new team at the University of Alabama at Birmingham (UAB), as well as Birmingham Barons baseball.

It's a good thing I like to travel. That year, I once made a twenty-one-day road trip to fifteen different cities, many of them far-flung. A typical week might look something like this: I would start out working the Bulls game in Winnipeg; then on their day off I would fly to Mobile for a UAB game against South Alabama; then to Edmonton for another Bulls game; then to Birmingham for UAB; then to Los Angeles for a Blues telecast. It was absolutely insane. But I loved it!

People often ask me if I have ever missed a game due to a canceled flight or other logistical snafu. Incredibly, I have not. I did have a very close call once. I had just done a Bulls game in Indianapolis, and the very next night the Blues were playing in Denver. There was terrible weather in both cities. Not much you can do about that! Thankfully, both airports finally opened, and I walked into the McNichols Sports Arena in Denver forty minutes before face-off.

Come to think of it, there have been some other close calls. One near-miss came years later, when I was doing the play-by-play for both the University of Alabama football and basketball teams. The football team was playing in the Blockbuster Bowl in Miami, while the very next night the basketball team was scheduled to open in a tournament in Honolulu.

We sent color analyst Tom Roberts to Hawaii to get things set up there while I went to Miami. The football game was a late start, 8:00 p.m., and it went long. There were a lot of time-outs, a lot of commercials, but eventually Alabama beat Colorado, and we wrapped things up. I got to bed around 1:00 a.m., then got up at 3:30 and caught a 6:00 a.m. flight to Honolulu by way of Dallas. This was a long flight— as far as you can physically travel in the United States—and I knew it was going to be very tight. If everything went perfectly, I would arrive at the game one hour prior to tip-off.

After landing, I bypassed the lovely ladies passing out leis and jumped into the first cab I saw. "University of Hawaii, please! The arena." But my driver didn't speak English. He just shrugged. I started gesturing like a guy shooting a basketball. The driver nodded. We arrived at the University of Hawaii arena, but it was deserted. Eventually we found someone who told us the game was at the Blaisdell Center. Downtown. We got back on the H-1 Expressway and sped toward downtown. I ran into the arena, still schlepping my suitcase and attaché case. Tom was already on the air, doing the pregame show. I sat down, mopped my brow, and ten minutes later was doing the game.

Alabama won that night. After the game, despite being in one of the most gorgeous places on earth, the beach on Waikiki, I stopped briefly at McDonald's, went to my room, collapsed, and went right to sleep.

Tom Roberts (L) and yours truly with the Bama basketball team at the Blaisdell Arena in Honolulu

With the exception of riding the bus for the Birmingham Barons from 1979 to 1983, and of course the occasional car trip, ever since I moved to Birmingham, the majority of my travel has been on planes. And I love planes.

People often complain about air travel, especially in this post-9/11 era. It can be a real hassle at times, but I still enjoy it. I guess it's because I spent so many years on those buses. I fly so much that I usually get upgraded to first class. It's actually ideal to work on the plane, since there are no phones and few distractions. I spend almost every flight making notes or editing audio on my laptop. I also like to read. I remember once back in 1993, I had just settled into my favorite seat, 1B, and opened a book I couldn't put down, *It Doesn't Take a Hero*, by General Norman Schwarzkopf.

I was deep into the book, having pretty much tuned out the other passengers filing onto the plane, when suddenly a shadow loomed over me and a booming voice said, "So, what do you think of that book?"

I started to answer before lifting my eyes. "It's really, really . . ." Then I looked up and saw the general himself standing there. Immediately, I got up so the commander of the Coalition Forces in the 1991 Gulf War could take his seat next to me. After he had settled into the window seat, I told him, "Sincerely, your book is spectacular."

"Glad you like it," he answered. "You're obviously a keen judge of literary talent." We both laughed, and he autographed the book for me. At that point he opened his attaché case to do a little work. I put his book away and began working on something I was very sad to have to do. NASCAR driver Alan Kulwicki had just died in a plane crash. During the broadcast at the upcoming race in Bristol, Tennessee, I would have to deliver the eulogy, so I was writing it out in order to get it just right. We both worked quietly until dinner was served; then we put our work away, enjoyed the meal, and talked the rest of the way to Atlanta.

Of course, I wasn't always on the road. I also found plenty to do close to home. In 1978, UAB, which previously had no intercollegiate sports program, hired former UCLA coach Gene Bartow to create the school's athletic department. Bartow, who also served as the school's first basketball coach (a position he ultimately held for eighteen years), wanted a new voice for his new franchise, so he hired me to do the basketball play-by-play. The team, the fans, the coach, and the broadcast crew were all rookies together. Everything was new.

It was a wonderful experience and a lot of fun. I was the new guy in a new market. Although I enjoyed doing the games, I had frequent

Engineer Jimmy Jones (L), Color man J.C. Dover (C), yours truly, and Butch Owens courtside for a UAB basketball broadcast

I'm with former UAB basketball coach and athletic director Gene Bartow upon my hiring as the first "voice" of the UAB Blazers.

scheduling conflicts with racing and hockey and ultimately had to choose to do all of the UAB games or none of them. So I stepped aside and handed off the microphone to Gary Sanders, who did the UAB broadcasts until he retired after the 2005–06 season.

Another opportunity that came my way after moving to Birmingham was local radio. As the Voice of the Bulls, I was periodically invited to be a guest on talk shows, including Dave Campbell's *The People Speak*, a local, five-night-a-week general topic talk show that covered sports on Friday nights. This led to my position as sports director at WERC radio.

At WERC, the first thing I did was put together a college scoreboard show called *The Calling All Sports Saturday Scoreboard*. In the late '70s and early '80s, these types of programs weren't nearly as prevalent as they are today. Cable TV was in its infancy, and we were still more than a decade away from the bombardment of sports Internet sites and blogs.

Although our show was the only one of its kind in Birmingham at the time, we didn't invent the genre. In fact, I based much of the format on old CBS radio shows such as Winn Elliott's *Sports Central USA*, where so-called correspondents around the country would contribute live reports. I did a few of these reports myself for Mutual Broadcasting when I was a kid calling in scores from the pay phone at Jets games!

During the week I would look at the schedule and arrange to get updates from the key college games, as well as some that were not in the national spotlight. I'd arrange with the sports information director at the school to have a correspondent call me collect after their game, then I would record their thirty-to-forty-second recap and play it later.

We'd go on the air with forty to forty-five cartridges (we called them *carts*) that looked like the broadcast version of 8-track tapes. We'd line them up alphabetically and play them after we talked about that particular game or if somebody called in asking for that score.

We always covered big games, such as Ohio State–Michigan or Alabama versus anyone. But I'd also be sure to hire a correspondent at Slippery Rock, because someone would always call in for the Slippery Rock score, just to be a wise guy.

In 1981 we also started a new sports call-in show, *Calling All Sports*. It's hard to believe, but this was a unique concept at the time! These days, these shows are everywhere. They should sell bumper stickers that say, "Honk if you have your own sports call-in show!" But ours was the first in Birmingham, and the show was soon syndicated throughout the state.

I was lucky. For most of the years that I did *Calling All Sports*, my programming was not influenced by ratings. The advertising was flying in, and we didn't have to be concerned about losing listeners because there was nowhere else for them to go! We were the only sports talk show around, so we weren't under pressure, like many

Former Arkansas Athletic Director and ABC Sports broadcaster Frank Broyles joins me on "Calling All Sports"

hosts are today, to put a lot of craziness on the air and partake in character assassination.

Not long ago, Paul Finebaum, a hugely successful sports talk show host in Birmingham, was interviewed in the *Birmingham News* about the current state of sports talk radio. He made the point that if he talked about the game between San Diego and Houston during his program, he would lose all his listeners. According to Finebaum, people want to talk about people. In other words, *gossip*. That's something I would not and will not do.

Back then, we focused on pure, straight sports and talked to some of the sporting world's biggest names. During the football season we broadcast the show from the Birmingham Touchdown Club meeting on Mondays, so we had access to their guest speakers. In addition, we interviewed NBA greats such as Charles Barkley, Julius Erving, and Muhammad Ali's trainer, Angelo Dundee, to name a few.

Other extraordinary guests included Dodgers manager Tommy Lasorda and then–Cincinnati Reds manager Sparky Anderson, who, incredibly, we put on the show two days before the biggest event in the state, the Alabama–Auburn football game. (These days, listeners wouldn't tolerate talking baseball during that particular week!)

Another magnificent guest was Mercury Morris, the former Miami Dolphins running back who spoke to us just a few hours after he was released from prison in May 1986. A few years prior, Morris had been convicted of cocaine trafficking and sentenced to twenty years. Then, after convincing a judge that his entrapment defense had been mistakenly excluded from the first trial, he was granted a retrial and released after reaching a plea bargain. The only other interviews he did that day were with the local media gathered outside the Florida correctional facility and with Larry King, who featured him as a guest on his radio program that evening. Through my contacts, we had Merc!

Willie Mays was another big name we had on the show. The first time he was scheduled to appear, we promoted it heavily. But he didn't show up. So when we rescheduled him, I didn't even mention that he was coming. When Willie walked into the studio, we played it like a wonderful surprise, as if former Alabamian (he was born in Westfield, Alabama) Willie Mays was in the neighborhood and dropped by for a chat.

Without a doubt, my most memorable day at WERC was January 26, 1983, the day the great University of Alabama football coach Paul W. "Bear" Bryant passed away. Incredibly, Bryant had just retired the month before, and no one could believe that this powerful, larger-than-life man was actually gone.

Upon learning the news, I broke into our regular programming with a bulletin announcing his passing. As it turned out, I wouldn't leave the airwaves until many hours later.

This was a huge story in Alabama. Businesses and schools closed. The phone lines were jammed. Basically, the entire state shut down. At WERC, we decided to broadcast the funeral live. This was way before CNN or, later, MSNBC commonly covered events like this. I for one had never participated in anything like this before.

Immediately, everyone in the newsroom sprang into action. We contracted with a traffic helicopter pilot to fly over the funeral procession as it made its way from Tuscaloosa to Birmingham, where Bryant would be buried, and give us reports. I proceeded to Elmwood Cemetery with reporter Tony Giles, who later became the public address announcer for University of Alabama football and basketball games. Giles went to the grave site, while I positioned myself near the gates to anchor the broadcast. Since we didn't have cell phones back then, Giles and I communicated via walkie-talkies. We did our very best to be respectful. We didn't do a play-by-play of the funeral by any means; we simply reported on who was coming and going from the cemetery ("Here comes the Texas coach, Darrell Royal, and his wife . . . There's the bus carrying the players from Coach Bryant's 1982 team . . . Folks, there are thousands of people gathered outside these gates, just to hear the service on the loudspeakers . . .") and talked to people when we could. Then, when the service began, we hushed up.

Back at the studio, we opened up the phones, and fans called in all day long to share their remembrances of Coach Bryant. We also aired interviews with dozens of famous sports (and nonsports) people. I don't think we missed anybody!

At one point we had three of the most successful college coaches ever—Darrell Royal, Bud Wilkinson, and Joe Paterno—all on the line at once, so we conferenced them together. All I had to say was, "Coach, you knew Coach Bryant for years. What can you tell us?"

I stayed on the air from noon till somewhere near midnight. The experience of that broadcast was incredible. But what stayed with me was the overall experience—the funeral, the emotion, the massive amount of media coverage. Where else would the death of a football coach get nonstop, statewide coverage? Truly the only things I can compare this event to are President Kennedy's funeral and the more recent coverage of the funeral of Pope John Paul II.

Rest in peace, coach.

The state of Alabama ground to a halt. What I found truly impressive was that on that day, it didn't matter whether you were an Auburn fan or an Alabama fan. Everyone mourned Coach Bryant.

In 1983 I had lived in Alabama for only five years. From the moment

I came to town, I knew Coach Bryant was important. But looking back, I don't think I truly understood what he meant to people until the day he died.

Working on the radio show eventually led to the opportunity to do sports on local TV. The folks at WBRC Channel 6, Birmingham's ABC affiliate at the time, were looking to make a change. After meeting with the news director, Lu Ann Reeb, I was offered the position of on-air sports director. We agreed that I would do the late news only, the 10:00 p.m. show.

The problem was, I knew next to nothing about TV! My only experience was one season working for the St. Louis Blues. I had no studio experience whatsoever. I didn't know how to edit videotape or how to write a script for TV. I was a radio play-by-play announcer and a sports radio talk show host, so I was used to ad-libbing and doing things off the cuff.

I used to hand in these scripts with notes regarding what graphics should appear behind me, but then when it came to highlights, I'd just say, "Roll Tape A." I didn't say, "Let's go to the videotape," because New York and Washington, D.C. sportscaster Warner Wolf pretty much owned that phrase. Instead, I'd say, "We'll take a look at the Jets and the Packers right here . . ."

Since I knew what was on the tape, I'd just ad-lib around the action, but the engineers weren't sure when to fade out of it and go to the next tape because I didn't write a full script. We worked through it, though, and I learned a lot, thanks to really helpful people such as Gil Tyree, who is now the sports director at the CBS affiliate in Atlanta, and who remains a dear friend, along with others, such as Ron Grillo and Jeff George.

Since I was already committed to doing NASCAR races and my

Tuesday evening program, *NASCAR Live!* for the Motor Racing Network (MRN), we compensated by sometimes doing my Channel 6 reports directly from the racetrack. There were many Friday nights when the anchorperson would say, "Eli's in Michigan this weekend, doing his NASCAR gig, but he's got the sports for us . . ." Then we'd converse back and forth during a live shot.

The MRN Radio crew from the 1980s, left to right are Dr. Jerry Punch, Ned Jarrett, Mike Joy, Barney Hall, and that peanut-selling kid from Brooklyn

One night I was doing the sports from a racetrack close to home, the Birmingham International Raceway, a short track that has turned out as many NASCAR stars as any other track in America. The timing was supposed to have worked out so that when the races were finished, I would go on the air for the late sports. But predictably enough, the race went long.

I was still standing next to the track when we went on the air. Subsequently, every time the cars came around in front of me, they totally obliterated my sound. You could hear me for half a lap; then, as the cars came back off turn four and back toward where I was standing, you could see my lips move, but the listeners never heard a word. There's one for the blooper reel!

During my two years with Channel 6, I also did a live call-in show, *Sports Talk with Eli*. The show was similar to the one I'd done on radio, *Calling All Sports*, except that we had one guest per show, and he or she would be live with us in the studio. We'd always open up with a short taped segment about the featured guest; then viewers would call in with questions.

My favorite guest on this show—and quite possibly the best interview I've ever done—was with the incredibly inspiring Eddie Robinson, the longtime football coach at Grambling State University, who passed away in 2007. When Robinson retired in 1997, he was the winningest coach in college football history, counting 408 wins during his fifty-six-year career. (Note to Bama fans: Coach Paul "Bear" Bryant held the title with 323 wins when he retired in 1982.)

Robinson coached some two hundred players who went on to careers in the NFL, including Super Bowl XXII MVP Doug Williams, who succeeded him as coach at Grambling in 1998 and led the Tigers to three consecutive Southwestern Athletic Conference titles during his tenure there.

The amazing thing to me was everything that Coach Robinson was able to achieve with very limited resources. Grambling State University, a small, historically black college in Grambling, Louisiana, did not have the budget or personnel of a large school, such as the University of Alabama. Yet Robinson set the bar high and kept winning against all odds.

The interview was so memorable not because of my questions but because of his answers, or rather, just the simple, powerful way he spoke. His life experience molded him into a man who confidently led a younger generation. That's what Coach Robinson was most proud of—the scores of young people he taught and influenced.

I learned a lot doing *Sports Talk with Eli*. Probably the most important thing I took away from the experience was not to overprepare for interviews. I mean, you have to prepare. But if you have your questions completely scripted out in advance, you tend not to go with the flow during the interview. If the host is really listening, every answer leads to another question. You sound stiff if you just read from a bullet-pointed list.

As much as I enjoyed my time at WBRC, I decided not to renew my contract after the second year. I had already started doing Bama games, plus I just wanted to travel more and really preferred covering live events. Besides, even though I've done a lot of TV, I really am basically a radio play-by-play guy with some sports-talk abilities. Especially at the time, I didn't consider myself a studio-TV kind of guy.

It's interesting how things come around, though. Years after I'd stopped hosting *Calling All Sports* on WERC radio, I was approached to do a new version of the program on WJOX-AM in Birmingham. Actually, we talked about doing the show for two or three years before I agreed. I was reluctant mainly because—as I mentioned earlier—I don't like the direction sports talk radio has taken. It's drivel. There are exceptions, of course. My buddy George Plaster does a terrific program, *The Sports Zone* on 104.5 in Nashville. But I'd rather listen to music or nothing than hear some guy yelling and arguing with a radio host.

Anyway, after I laid down some ground rules—I refused to talk about recruiting, speculate on coaching changes, or otherwise engage in any conversations that would jeopardize my position as the Voice of the Crimson Tide—they made me an offer I couldn't refuse. Against my better judgment, I did the show for just one year.

First, I was excited with all the new technology. Unlike the previous incarnation of the show, this time I could broadcast directly from my home! Also, I truly think we put on a good show. As in the early days, we had some top-notch guests. Over the years I'd built up a pretty good Rolodex, and that worked to our advantage. For instance, the day the Yankees signed A-Rod, the Yankees' management walked off the stage, picked up the phone, and called my talk show!

The ratings were good too. We even beat Rush Limbaugh! Still, for a number of reasons, I decided to let it go. I'm not a guy to ever say never. Under the right circumstances, I might do another talk show. But for now, I have more than enough talking to do. And I'm grateful for that.

NINE

I Can Do That, Can't I?

ONE SUNDAY AFTERNOON DURING 1975, WHEN LAPELS AND TIES were wide and the hot new car on the road was the AMC Pacer, I was riding down a Southern highway on a minor-league hockey team's bus, looking for a way to pass the time. I grabbed my little transistor radio, put the plug in my ear, and flipped the dial until I picked up a signal. What do you know? A NASCAR race.

I liked racing. I'd seen it on TV from time to time, although the coverage I saw was usually limited to ten minutes of black-and-white highlights from Daytona or Darlington on *Wide World of Sports*. They'd run a clip of a big crash or a checkered-flag moment sandwiched in between the wrist-wrestling from Petaluma, California, and the Duke Kahanamoku Surfing Classic from Hawaii.

I didn't even know that NASCAR races were broadcast on the radio. I never heard one growing up in Brooklyn. But I liked what I heard and couldn't help but think, *I can do that, can't I?*

When I heard the announcer say, "This is the Motor Racing Network . . ." I wrote down the name and initials, MRN. Then when I got home, I called them. Their offices at Daytona International Speedway were relatively small back then, compared to the operation of today, and I immediately got through to Tim Sullivan, the man who was running the network at the time. I started pestering him for a job. When Jack Arute took over as general manager, I pestered him too. One day, Arute, who now works for ABC and ESPN and remains one of the best pit reporters in the business, took one of my many calls and asked me a very reasonable question. "Have you done any racing before?"

I said, "Of course I have!"

This was a fib—OK, a full-blown lie—since I had never even been to a racetrack before.

Arute inquired further. "What did you do?"

I couldn't be so bold as to say I'd done radio before, so I told him I had worked as a public address announcer.

He said, "Send me some of your tapes."

Well, now I was in a jam, because the tapes didn't exist. After a few days I called him back and told him I couldn't find my racing tapes, but I'd be happy to send along some of my hockey tapes.

By this time it was early 1976. I was the play-by-play announcer for the Hampton Gulls and was just a year and a half away from my first NHL job with the St. Louis Blues. I was doing a pretty good hockey broadcast. I was confident in that product. So I sent him a tape of a hockey game, and he called me back to say he thought it was very good. I guess Jackie figured if I could keep up with the pace of hockey, which is tremendously fast, then I could keep up with the pace of racing, because he gave me my first assignment.

"We'll send you to Charlotte in May over Memorial Day weekend and put you on the air," Jackie said. "If you do well, we'll keep you. If you stink, we'll send you home."

Today, it is absolutely unheard-of to be offered an on-air audition for a NASCAR race, or any sports broadcast, for that matter. Aspiring broadcasters have to work their way up from a first job at a short track in Hutchaplutch, North Carolina, then jump through all kinds of hoops to even get a shot at any sort of a network job. The thing was, this type of tryout wasn't all that outrageous in the mid-'70s. NASCAR had yet to explode into the force it has become, and people weren't exactly beating down the door to work the radio broadcasts. So I was bound for the World 600 in Charlotte (now called the Coca-Cola 600) to do my first race.

The first thing I did was get a tape of the broadcast of the World 600 from the previous year. I listened to that tape constantly. Every time I was in the car, I'd pop in the ol' 8-track and listen to nothing but the World 600. I'd study the phrases they used and the pacing. Before I went to Charlotte, I had no idea how to describe a race, but I learned how to do so from that tape.

On race weekend, May 1976, I was on the air at Charlotte Motor Speedway, working Turns One and Two of the broadcast.

Before the race everyone was talking about the big promotion for that weekend. The president of the track, Humpy Wheeler, whose name would become synonymous with innovative promotions, was awarding the driver who led the first lap with the unbelievable bonus of a thousand dollars!

The only similarity between the Charlotte Motor Speedway of 1976 and today's Lowe's Motor Speedway is the actual ribbon of asphalt. Everything else has been upgraded and redone.

Smiling for the camera in the late 80s

Back then, there was a section of seats in Turn One and another in Turn Four; and above that section was a tower section of seats that were covered by a hard roof. My position was on top of that roof in Turn One. It was an amazing view!

I was nervous before I got there, but once I climbed up to the roof, the nerves really set in. These days we use wireless technology with backup systems. Even the backups have backups. But in 1976 we lived a little more dangerously. Everything was hard-wired into place. We used to bring a battery-powered, wire-filled box up to the turn with us and literally plug it into an old, four-pronged telephone jack. The dry pair, as we called it, was a wire going through the roof in Turn One and back to our equipment on the ground.

Live races wouldn't be seen on TV until 1979, but one TV station was doing a partial telecast at Charlotte that day. So, a half hour before we were due to go on the air, the TV truck fired up the last of their equipment, and *boom!*—the whole press box shut down. A total power outage. I was out in Turn One, and since I was wired to the press box, my headset went dead. I had no idea why.

I started pacing the roof, thinking, *What am I going to do? What am I going to do?*

After about three minutes, which felt much more like three eternities, the power came back on. The good thing was the power outage caused such an adrenaline surge that I had no time to further obsess about this being my first race.

Once I was connected, I was beyond relieved to hear the voices of Ken Squier and Jack Arute in the booth and Barney Hall in Turns Three and Four. The rest of our crew that day consisted of Charlie Harville, who was a sports anchor for a TV station in the Greensboro market; Bob Myers, who went on to become an outstanding magazine writer; and Joe Aloia, another pit reporter.

As for me, I just called the action. I didn't speculate about what was wrong with somebody's car. I didn't try to pass myself off as Mr. Motorsports. I just called it like I saw it.

I made a very conscious effort to keep it simple and try not to cram ten pounds of stuff into a five-pound-bag. I knew I had a lot to learn.

After the race Barney Hall and I went downstairs and walked out to our cars. No one was getting out of there anytime soon—traffic was crawling—so we got some fried chicken and sat just like a couple of tailgating fans, right there in the parking lot.

While eating, I asked Barney, whom I would have the pleasure of sitting beside as coanchor in the near future, "So, how'd I do?"

"Not bad," he said with a smile. "Not bad."

With the old Daytona broadcast tower in the background, the MRN crew in the mid 80s was (L-R) yours truly, Ned Jarrett, Mike Joy and Barney Hall.

As a turn announcer, you are about as close to the action as you can get without driving a race car or working as a jack man in the pits. I always felt especially up close and personal at Pocono.

The racetrack at Pocono is triangular-shaped with a nine-tenth's-mile-long front straightaway. A 747 can literally take off from that particular stretch; it's the longest one on a NASCAR track. Banking at this track is limited, but there is one relatively high-banked turn, the high-speed hairpin Turn One, right at the end of that long front straightaway.

During the Pocono Winston Cup race of 1982, I was positioned at the apex of Turn One, atop a tall, wooden scaffold partially covered by a big piece of wood painted to look like a giant pack of Winston cigarettes. In the middle of the race, Dale Earnhardt and Tim Richmond got into a tangle. They were off the asphalt, onto the grass, and back onto the asphalt; then they crashed on the main straightaway, spinning wildly down that long stretch. Earnhardt's car flipped on its side and started tumbling right toward me in Turn One. I was describing all this on the air when—*bam!*—his car slammed into my broadcast tower, and an enormous piece of sheet metal came flying in my direction like a guillotine Frisbee. The thing darn near decapitated me! I ducked and kept talking. I figured if I was going to die, I'd go down talking.

Earnhardt's car landed on its back, upside down, leaking oil. Of course, there was a red flag, and although Earnhardt was hopping on one foot as Richmond helped him across the track, both drivers were ultimately fine.

When the race was over, I went out into the woods behind the turn position and retrieved that piece of sheet metal. I still have it—the whole fender, the entire sheet metal assembly from Earnhardt's car! It's on display in my office.

After that race I covered a few more Pocono races from that position. During a USAC race later that same year, Eldon Rasmussen was coming down the straightaway in his baby blue Indy car and something malfunctioned—I think the wing came loose—causing him to lose control. Right at the apex of the turn, he slammed into the wall, which was right at the base of my broadcast tower. I was showered with shards of light blue fiberglass. (Rasmussen and I were both fine).

During the next couple of NASCAR races at Pocono, I worked from that same tower in Turn One, which I should report has since been moved a few feet out of the turn. I'd look for Earnhardt during the pace lap before the race would begin. He would drive up the banking, lean around the roll bar in the car, look up at me, and wave as he drove past, as if to say, "OK, you stay out of my car, and I'll stay out of your broadcast tower."

There's nothing funny about wrecks. Believe me, having been around racing for over thirty-five years, I know this for certain. But accidents are part of life on the racetrack. One of the funniest stories I've ever heard involves Buddy Baker's accident at the old Smoky Mountain Raceway.

Buddy, whom I worked with on TNN's NASCAR broadcasts during the late '90s, gathered heaps of accolades during his racing career, including being named one of NASCAR's 50 Greatest Drivers back in 1998. But as every driver does now and again, Buddy was having a bad day and slammed his car head-on into the wall, breaking a couple of his ribs.

Immediately, the ambulance came to collect him and take him to the local hospital. Things got off to a rocky start, though, when the paramedic—or maybe he was the paramedic's cousin driving the ambulance—tried to pull Buddy out of the car by his head. According to Buddy, the guy, whom he nicknamed Barney Fife, weighed about 140 pounds and couldn't even budge Buddy, who tipped the scales at around 225.

Eventually they got Buddy out of the car, strapped him onto the gurney, slid him into the back of the ambulance, and shut the doors. This was not your typical short track. Because of the terrain, you actually had to run uphill on the back straightaway while you ran downhill on the front stretch. Also, at this track, you had to physically cross the racetrack to get to the gate that exited onto the service road. There was no underground tunnel at this little country track.

The race was under caution due to Buddy's accident, so when Barney Fife spotted an opening, he gunned it up the hill to get to the crossover gate. What he didn't know was that the attendants hadn't shut the ambulance doors completely, nor had they properly locked the gurney into place. So when he accelerated toward the gate, the doors flew open, and Buddy, still strapped to the gurney, came shooting out of the back of the ambulance like a bullet. It was like the luge competition at the Grenoble Olympics!

Now Buddy was rolling downhill on the back straightaway! He was trying to maneuver the gurney by leaning and using his body weight but became understandably agitated when he saw cars on the horizon. He managed to free one of his arms from under the strap and waved wildly, hoping someone would notice him. Cars were coming out of the turn, whizzing by him, but luckily the gurney listed to the side and ran into the mud. The gurney flipped over, and Buddy landed in some bushes, sustaining more scratches and bruises than he did during his wreck.

"Good thing I was strapped to that gurney," Buddy said. "Otherwise I would have kicked the crap out of Barney Fife that day."

Working for MRN during those first few years was akin to being part of a MASH unit. We had to be mobile. Just like today, every weekend we'd travel to a track, set up, break down, then move on to the next track. These days, the MRN engineering crew travels in big trucks, fifty-three-foot transporters with complete, compact radio stations configured on the inside. In the late '70 s and early '80s, all the MRN equipment fit into a van. We had just upgraded from a station wagon, so we were really proud of that van!

Happy to be working in Daytona

Besides being mobile, we had to be adaptable. We learned to expect the unexpected and figure out a solution. Fast.

For a few years NASCAR ran races at the Texas World Speedway in Bryan, Texas (not to be confused with today's Texas Motor Speedway in Fort Worth). Our first trip there, I arrived a few days early to help our engineer, Harry Howard, set up the equipment. Back then, we had little to no support staff, so that particular weekend it was up to me and Harry, a brilliant guy who used to work for NASA, to get the equipment up and running.

For this race the broadcast tower was located at the top of a large hill near the start/finish line. In order to drive up to the top of the hill, which you really needed to do if you had a lot of equipment, the track required you to obtain something they imaginatively called a "hill pass." Literally, it was a piece of white paper with the word *hill* printed on it.

For some reason, the credentials office, which was in complete disarray, refused to give Harry a hill pass.

We were faced with the possibility of having to haul a lot of gear nearly a mile, and we weren't going to do that. While walking past the area near the press box, I saw a truck with a hill pass dangling from its windshield, flapping in the wind. Then, with God as my witness, the hill pass flew off that windshield and landed directly in my hands. I swear it happened.

Without sharing the particulars of my divine intervention with Harry, I just told him, "Hey, I got a pass."

Time to go to work. We went to the van, stuck the pass on our windshield, and drove toward the tower, where they waved us in. Immediately, we loaded our equipment on the elevator and began setting up for the weekend.

A few days passed. It was now Sunday, and we were having our prerace production meeting in the press box, when suddenly, a six-foot-nine Texas lawman walked in the door and said, in a menacing growl, "Who owns that van out there?"

Somebody spoke up and said it was our network van.

"Where'd ya get that pass from?"

Nobody spoke. I considered coming clean. But do you really think he would have believed me if I said it had flown into my hands? Visions of the Steep Hollow, Texas, lockup were dancing in my head. So I remained silent. Then Harry, who could have ratted me out, said something like, "I think they gave it to us when we checked in."

Well, the pass was numbered, so the trooper knew it belonged to a van from the P&N Plumbing Company. But we were already in. The pass was yesterday's problem. Long gone. We had moved on to worrying about the next concern, which at the moment was how to ignore mosquitoes that were so big they needed a flight attendant on board.

Part of being adaptable is dealing with all the changes in technology. And there have been many during the last thirty years. I'm lucky; being a gadget geek, I've embraced the changes. But every time something new comes along, you always need time to iron out the kinks.

At the racetrack, we used to communicate through telephone lines and wires, which ran from each of our positions around the racetrack, to the press box, and into the control board. Those of us working the turns or the pits were literally wired into place. This made for some logistical challenges. For instance, Ned Jarrett, the NASCAR champion–turned–MRN commentator, used to interview drivers when they dropped out of the race due to an accident or equipment failure. Since Ned couldn't leave his broadcast position, he would send runners to ask drivers if they would please come talk to Ned at his post. This could be daunting, especially if the driver was way across the track or, even worse, was ticked off following a wreck.

The runners would literally chase the drivers down. Most of the time the drivers cooperated—they knew the drill—but if they were mad or frustrated or if they got interrupted en route, Ned was out of luck. Wireless technology changed all that. We were no longer tethered to our positions. Mohammad no longer had to come to the mountain. On-air guys could go directly to the drivers for interviews.

Wireless technology was a major improvement, but the first time we used it at Daytona, we kept picking up the communications from the drive-through at the Burger King on Volusia Avenue (now International Speedway Boulevard). I'm accustomed to having several voices in my ear at once during a broadcast, but it was unusual to be describing a driver moving in from the back of the pack while hearing, "I'll have a Number Four, no pickles, no onions, and a Diet Coke."

This problem would continue to pop up over the years. Once, Alabama played a football game against Ole Miss in Jackson, Mississippi, where Jackson Memorial Stadium was located directly across from a hospital. We had wireless communications between the press box and the sidelines, but between updates from our sideline reporter, we kept hearing, "Dr. Johnson! Room 301. Stat!"

These days there are so many people on wireless frequencies that at major sporting events it can get to be a seriously tangled web. The NFL actually employs a frequency coordinator! At the Daytona 500, there might be twenty-five TV stations doing local shots back to their communities. Then there's network TV and radio. Just before the race, the engineers will think they have everything settled, and somebody will fire up a piece of equipment to interrupt the signal. Thankfully, though, 99.9 percent of the time, our crack technical team has everything running like a top by airtime.

Another innovation that blossomed from wireless technology

was miking drivers during the race. It didn't always work at first, but we did get a great piece of audio from Dick Brooks, the ebullient driver from California who went on to become an excellent MRN pit reporter.

Dick came off Turn Four in Talladega and got into a big ol' wreck. He was tumbling and stumbling and spinning while we were watching, holding our collective breath. As soon as he stopped, he keyed the radio and said, "Well, boys, hope you enjoyed that ride as much as I did." Magnificent stuff.

That was the infancy of radio communication in NASCAR. Back then, many teams still communicated with chalkboards and hand signals! Teams would set up signals ahead of time, so if your driver put his hand out his car window and pointed to the front, it meant he wanted two new tires. If the car was loose or pushing, they'd have a signal for that. It's hard to imagine, but that system got the job done for decades.

There's one thing that even technology can't control: the weather. At racetracks, which are uncovered and exposed to the elements, rain and even snow and ice often present an issue. Races are always delayed or halted when the track is wet because NASCAR race cars run on tires with no tread. Even the least little bit of wetness on the racetrack can cause even a heavy stockcar to hydroplane. Trust me: a hydroplaning high-speed stock car is not good. Because of that caution, we're used to delays.

In 1996 I began doing race telecasts for The Nashville Network (TNN), which included coverage of World of Outlaws (WoO) events, among its many offerings. The World of Outlaws is a sanctioning body overseeing two national dirt track touring series, including the Late Model Series, which features late-model stock cars, and the

Sprint Cup Series, which features high-powered, custom fabricated sprint cars, unmistakable for their large, adjustable wings and oversized rear tires.

My TNN Motorsports booth mates Buddy Baker (L) and Dr. Dick Berggren (R) were two of the best that I've ever had the pleasure of working with.

One night we did a race at the Eldora Speedway in New Weston, Ohio, a track now owned by NASCAR champion Tony Stewart. The place, which holds some eighteen thousand fans in the seats plus however many they can fit on the hillside, was packed to the gills. When we got to the track, hours before the start of the race, it was raining, and it continued raining. It was also extremely hot and muggy, especially in the broadcast booth, which had no air-conditioning. Our statistician/assistant, Martha Oliver, and later, yours truly, spent hours sitting in the small, unisex restroom because it was the only place with AC! Oddly enough, the bathroom was also the place they stored the championship trophy.

As the evening wore on, the track officials refused to call the event. The thing was, virtually none of the fans left the venue. They were happy. The racetrack concessionaires, who were selling tons of hot dogs and plenty of beer, were happy. A few fans went out to their cars to take naps, but if anyone left, I didn't see it. Finally, at 2:00 in the morning the races began. They concluded around 4:00 a.m., which was just enough time for us to zip back to the hotel, grab our suitcases, and make our 6:00 a.m. flight home.

I spent another profoundly rainy weekend at the Texas World Speedway, working for MRN. Qualifying had been rained out early, so everyone went back to the hotel. This was in the days before fancy motor coaches were commonplace, so during this race weekend, it seemed as if absolutely everyone involved with the race—from drivers to crew guys to broadcasters—was staying at the local Ramada Inn.

One of the hotel guests was country music singer and part-time NASCAR driver Marty Robbins, who was competing in that weekend's race. Robbins was genuinely a good driver and used to drive this purple and lime green car prepared by a gentleman named Cotton Owens. He didn't compete enough to really win big, but he was talented. His driving wasn't just a gimmick.

That day, everyone ended up in the hotel's cocktail lounge, which the hotel manager had generously opened early to accommodate folks returning from the track. Robbins got up on the stage with his guitar and started singing. Unplugged! He sang "El Paso" and "Don't Worry," and a bunch of other songs I couldn't name, but he entertained us for over two hours, and it was wonderful.

Since qualifying had been rained out, the drivers started Sunday's race based on their points. In other words, they lined up according to their overall standing in the season so far. The race started late because it was still raining. Everything was a mess. At one point, Cecil Gordon, a driver who later went on to become part of Dale Earnhardt's championship winning crew, spun off the racetrack into the infield grass area and sank in the mud. It was so muddy that they sent a wrecker in to get him, and the wrecker sank in the mud! So another wrecker came out to pull out the first wrecker; then they pulled out Cecil Gordon.

When races go long, there is a domino effect. All the people involved with the event are late to the next event. Or maybe they're just late going home. Which after a long, rainy weekend, you're really ready to do.

That particular evening, many of us were running late and in danger of missing our flights out of Houston. These were the days before most drivers or team owners had their own private aircraft.

A group of us were leaving the track in a mad rush to get to the airport, and, somehow, I ended up driving the rental car belonging to David Pearson—yes, *that* David Pearson: the NASCAR champion famous for his rivalry with Richard Petty.

As I drove a big Crown Victoria, my coanchor, Barney Hall, sat next to me. In the back were Pearson, Ned Jarrett, and team owner, Bud Moore. All this magnificent driving talent in the car and I was behind the wheel! Well, we were seriously late, and I was driving like a . . . how does that old saying go? *If you don't like my driving, then stay off the sidewalk.*

Barney was silent (no doubt muttering his prayers), but the other guys were egging me on: "Go over there! Try the median! Faster! Faster!"

Soon, we came screeching into the airport, with mere minutes to spare. There was no time to return the car and still make the flight, so as we were pulling up to the curb, I looked at Pearson in the rearview mirror and asked, "What do you want to do with the car?"

He said, "Stop and pop the trunk. And the hood."

So I stopped and popped the hood and the trunk. While Barney, Ned, and Bud scrambled to get the luggage out of the trunk, Pearson reached underneath the hood of the car and tugged on a cluster of wires. Then he and I grabbed our stuff. We left the car and ran through the airport (no security in those pre-9/11 days), making it to our plane as the doors were about to close. Once on board, Pearson looked at me and said, "Remind me to call Avis when we get to Atlanta to tell them their car died right in front of the airport."

Come to think of it, getting to and from the racetracks was at least half the fun. Once it became more commonplace for drivers to own their own planes, sometimes guys would be gracious enough to offer me a lift home. The most generous in this regard were Davey and Bobby Allison, who lived near my home in Birmingham.

The Allisons, along with drivers Neil Bonnett and Red Farmer, were referred to as the "Alabama Gang." They used to fly in and out of the small airport in Bessemer, Alabama, or as they called it, "Hueytown International Airport," so named for their nearby hometown of Hueytown, Alabama (a western suburb of Birmingham).

Bobby was an outstanding pilot. In fact, he had been a test pilot for the Piper Corporation and always had these cutting-edge airplanes. He had access to the newest type of engines, courtesy of the Allison (no relation) Engine Company, and would install them on his plane the moment they were approved by the FAA. Since this new equipment was deemed experimental, his plane would include an X in the call letters, N12BAX: N (the call letter for American aircraft), 12 (his car number), BA (his initials), and X (experimental).

Often, if there was a seat available, Bobby would invite me to fly home with him. He also made a habit of bringing along other drivers. It was not unusual for a driver to fly home with Bobby to get some equipment that Bobby no longer needed. This could be a treasure to an underfinanced driver! Rather than throw it away, Bobby was more than happy to give it to someone who needed it.

On one particular flight, Dave Marcis came along to collect some equipment from Bobby's shop. He'd never flown with Bobby before. But I had.

Bobby had a ritual, something he did at the end of almost every flight. Especially after a victory.

Invariably, we'd be over Anniston, Alabama, and Bobby would identify himself to air traffic control: "November one two bravo alpha, twenty-eight thousand feet . . ." After the controller established the heading, he would ask, "How'd it go today, Bobby?"

Bobby would answer, "We did OK. We won!"

Then Bobby always looked back toward his passengers and said, "Time to do the victory lap."

He then tipped the nose, flipped the plane over, and flew home upside down. This wasn't just a stunt roll. We flew the final fifteen minutes completely inverted!

The first time I rode with him, he asked me ahead of time if I was strapped in. I was and made it a point always to buckle up when flying with Bobby. However, Dave Marcis was not so lucky.

As we flew overhead Anniston, heading toward Bessemer, Bobby tipped the plane. Neil Bonnett, who was also on the plane and had fallen asleep, was jolted awake. He had flown with Bobby many times, though, so he knew the drill. But Marcis, who was not wearing a seat belt, proceeded to fly through the cabin and kind of roll around until we landed. It truly was one of the funniest things I've ever seen.

On the ground, Bobby brought the plane to a stop and said what he always said: "Well, we cheated death again."

Beats flying commercial.

TEN

Tuesdays with Eli

I DIDN'T SEE IT COMING. WHEN I STARTED WORKING FOR MRN and NASCAR in 1976, I had no idea that the sport would explode into the three-billion-dollars-a-year behemoth that it is today. There are many reasons for this. But first and foremost, the success of NASCAR is due to the drivers.

As a sport that sprang up from the rural South, many of the drivers, especially from the old days, tended to come from humble beginnings, working their way up through the ranks, beginning with dirt tracks and drag races. Many of the drivers of today, both Northerners and Southerners alike, still hail from small towns and as a rule tend to be polite and down-to-earth.

From the sport's earliest days, NASCAR drivers were accessible to the fans. Although that's changed a bit, stock-car drivers remain the most fan-friendly in all of sports.

On *NASCAR Live!*, the Tuesday night call-in show I've hosted since 1983, fans call in to ask questions and talk to their favorite drivers. This is still the only NASCAR show where fans can speak directly to the guest, who can be anyone from the president of NASCAR to last week's winner of the Daytona 500.

The show began simply enough.

I had been working for MRN, doing race broadcasts for several years, when NASCAR vice president Jim Foster, and our general manager, John McMullin, came up with the idea of doing a talk show back when everybody and his brother weren't doing sports talk. At the time, I had been hosting a general sports call-in show, *Calling All Sports*, on WERC radio in Birmingham, for just over a year. Since I had some experience with this format, I was given a shot at hosting *NASCAR Live!*

We started on twenty-five stations, and as of 2008, which was our twenty-fifth anniversary, *NASCAR Live!* was heard on some 456 stations. It also became accessible to subscribers of Sirius XM Radio, which means that NASCAR fans in less-populated states, such as Montana or Wyoming, can now hear the show.

From the start, drivers were very responsive. We've never had trouble getting guests (see aforementioned accessibility). They understood that we were—and still are—giving them a valuable opportunity to sell themselves and their sponsor.

On the air at the Darlington Raceway with Hall-Of-Famer Cale Yarborough

We've never had trouble getting callers, either. I mean, what racing fan doesn't want to pick up the phone and talk directly to Matt Kenseth or Tony Stewart? And who would have guessed when we started the show that I would only have to use the dump button (the switch that hangs up on a caller and prevents what he just said from being heard on the air) four times

I don't know what I said that night in Daytona, but I had driver Bill Elliott and Ken Squier of CBS Sports listening closely.

in twenty-five years! I have been pleasantly surprised to learn that the callers are very respectful of each guest, even if they aren't fans of a particular driver. Sure, sometimes callers will say, "Why'd you do that?" or "What were you thinking?" But as a rule, they're never rude or confrontational.

We did run into one problem early on, though. Our phone number on the show is 1-800-2NASCAR.

As it turned out, a lot of folks were dialing 1-800-NASCAR2. An easy mistake.

But the thing is, the letter *N* on the phone shares the same push button as the letter *M*. And the number 2 shares the button with the letter *A*. So, if you dialed 1-800-NASCAR2, you were also dialing 1-800-MASCARA, which was the toll-free number for a makeup company.

Every Tuesday night between 7:00 and 8:00 p.m. EST, this makeup company was getting flooded with calls from people who wanted to talk to Richard Petty. The makeup people got pretty irritated, but we were excited so many calls were coming in. Soon enough, folks got the number right.

I couldn't begin to list all the memorable guests we've had on the show over the years—from Richard Petty, Dale Earnhardt, and Cale Yarborough to Jeff Gordon, Kyle Busch, and Kevin Harvick. I can't think of a driver we haven't had. One of the early standouts, though, was Junior Johnson.

Not only was Johnson one of NASCAR's early superstars (he won fifty NASCAR races during his career); he remained active in the sport after retiring as a driver and became a hugely successful car owner. He was one of racing's most colorful characters and one of the very best storytellers I've ever met.

Many of NASCAR's pioneers, including Johnson, honed their driving skills while running moonshine in the hills of North Carolina. They'd soup up their cars to outrun the revenuers over mountaintops and on backwoods roads. Johnson's family maintained a shop up in the holler where on one side of the wall they built cars to outrun the revenuers, and on the other side of the wall they built cars for the local police force.

At the time of our interview, it was common knowledge that Johnson had been to prison. He was later pardoned by President Reagan in 1986, but at the time, all I knew was that he'd served time in prison. I didn't know the particulars. One evening he called in from his home to be a guest on the program. (Guests are seldom in the studio. The wonders of technology!) He and I talked for a bit, then we opened the phone lines. A call came in from Chillicothe, Ohio. I said, "Chillicothe, hello! You're on the air with Junior Johnson!"

The caller asked a rather ordinary question, Johnson answered, and we went to a commercial. Off the air Junior said to me, "I don't mind telling ya, that's about as uncomfortable as I've ever been in my own living room."

I said, "What do you mean?"

"Chillicothe, Ohio," Junior said. "That's where I went to college."

I said, "Excuse me?"

He said, "Chillicothe! College! Or as you might call it, Federal Prison."

Well, I hadn't realized that Chillicothe, Ohio, was where he served eleven months of a two-year sentence for moonshining back in 1957.

"When you said Chillicothe, Ohio, I didn't know if it was one of my old cellmates or someone who knew me up there," Johnson said. "For a few seconds, it took my breath away."

We didn't discuss Johnson's prison days on the air, but a few years later we did discuss his latest business venture, Junior Johnson's Midnight Moon—a triple-distilled, 80-proof Carolina Moonshine product that is sold in ABC stores. Legally! He also produces a line of fried pork skins, but no doubt about it, the moonshine on the shelf of your local liquor store completes the Junior Johnson legend.

It's not just the old guard keeping this show afloat. A recent guest was young Joey Logano, who in 2009 became the youngest driver (at age eighteen) to compete in the Daytona 500. Among other things, we talked about his family traveling with him to races and the fact that his mother often gets too nervous to watch him on the track but still prefers her son racing to playing football.

Carl Edwards was a guest in 2008, when each week we played a flashback interview to celebrate the twenty-fifth anniversary of the show. During that particular show, the flashback featured Richard Petty and his decision not to put his name over his car door, as was the custom. He and his team were trying to establish the value of the STP colors and the 43 number, so they left off the name. When we finished playing the clip and shifted to Edwards, he said the Petty factoid was news to him.

Jokingly, I said, "You should have been listening to the show, Carl."

He said, "I did! I always listened to your show when I was growing up."

I guess we have been around for a while.

NASCAR Live! listeners know their stuff, and callers inquire often about automotive technology—engines, fuel, horsepower, shocks, and so forth. Often I won't know the answer to a question. When that's the case, I'll say so, then find someone who does. For instance, not long ago a guy called in asking about the positioning of the exhaust pipes on the new car. I didn't know the answer. So I sent a producer a message to call John Darby, the NASCAR Sprint Cup Series director. We got the answer from him, and I relayed it to the listeners. I'm not going to pretend I know something when I don't!

As much as callers enjoy technical talk, the show isn't limited to discussions of racetrack conditions or the intricacies of restrictor plate racing. Often, it gets personal.

Jeff Gordon talked about putting his newborn baby to bed. Ryan Newman shared the passion that he and his wife, Krissie, have for saving animals. Tony Stewart confessed to being clueless when it comes to shopping, and enlisting the help of a female friend to help him buy clothes. Dale Earnhardt Jr. shared how much fun it was to run the bulldozer when he helped with the demolition of his former house, which he tore down to make room for a new one. And team owner Jack Roush discussed how the painful recovery he endured after his 2002 plane crash made him determined to, as he put it, "make my remaining days on earth count."

After doing a show fifty-two weeks a year for twenty-six years

NASCAR greats Jeff Gordon (L) and Cale Yarborough (R) flank me during a talk show at the Darlington Raceway

Dale Earnhardt, Jr. (also seated) is about to join me on a talk show in Daytona.

now, one thing I've learned is that you always learn something. Recently, Jimmie Johnson was taken to the emergency room after cutting himself at the racetrack. I couldn't imagine how that had happened. So when he came on the show, he shared the particulars.

"Those race cars are really hot, so we wear a cool suit underneath; cool air kind of pumps through the tubes in the suit," Johnson said. "You have to get the cold air out of the suit. So, we take the suit down, poke a hole in the pocket, and fish the tubes out and plug them into the machine. I was in the process of doing that, and I knew I was going to cut myself because I had the blade pointing down at my leg. I knew it was coming and wasn't smart enough to stop! I put the knife over, and as I went to cut through, the blade cut my middle finger and the tendon."

It hurts just talking about it!

Unfortunately, some of the most memorable shows are those that follow a tragedy. Accidents and fatalities are a sad reality in NASCAR. But that's the thing about racing. You love the competition, you love the people, but this is a sport where the competitors could pay the ultimate price. That's one reason why NASCAR is set apart from other sports. If you make an error on the baseball field, they put the letter *E* up on the scoreboard. If you fumble the football, the other team might gain possession of the ball. But in NASCAR, a driver could pay for a mistake with his life.

In May 2000, nineteen-year-old Adam Petty was killed during a practice lap at the New Hampshire International Speedway, as it was known in those days, the day before he was scheduled to compete in a Busch Series race at that same track. Obviously, the NASCAR community and the Petty family were devastated. Adam was the first fourth-generation driver in NASCAR history, following his great-grandfather Lee; his grandfather Richard; and his father, Kyle, into the sport. He was a rising star when he lost his life, and he will always be greatly missed.

After a respectful period of time had passed, I contacted Adam's parents, Kyle and Patty Petty, to invite them on the program. They were very receptive because they wanted to honor their son and also reach millions of NASCAR fans, many of whom had been showering them with well wishes and support.

During a show like this, we do not take phone calls. We wouldn't want to put the guest on the spot, and in a sensitive situation, it's better that I guide the interview. The show was emotional, but the Pettys were prepared for it. On the positive side, we spent a great deal of time talking about their dream of building the Victory Junction Camp, a facility for chronically ill children that was in the development stages when Adam died. The Pettys turned something horrific—the untimely death of their son—into an incredible legacy. The Victory Junction Camp, which they dedicated to Adam's memory, did indeed become a reality when it opened in Randleman, North Carolina, in 2004, and this tremendous place continues to be a haven for sick children and their families.

I remember so many more good interviews than bad ones, but one guest I could not get to loosen up was Terry Labonte. He's a wonderful guy, but I've never had a good interview with him! This surprised me because even though he's a private person, I got to know him pretty well when we worked together during IROC (International Race of Champions) events, in addition to the NASCAR races. I was the public address announcer for IROC, and Labonte was a driver/participant. We flew to and from the events together on a private plane and laughed and told jokes the whole time. Then, on a Tuesday night I had him on NASCAR Live! and it was like pulling teeth! Looking back, I wonder if I didn't ask the right questions. Or maybe he was uncomfortable with the fact that on this show, you don't have any advance warning of what the next question will be. Some people find that somewhat daunting. The Wood brothers certainly did.

For years I tried to get NASCAR pioneers Leonard and Glen Wood on the show. Leonard is the legendary mechanic who, along with his brother, Glen, founded the storied Wood Brothers Racing team in 1949. Over the years, some of the biggest names in racing competed for the Wood brothers, including Dale Jarrett, Cale Yarborough, A.J. Foyt, and David Pearson, who claimed forty-three checkered flags driving the Number 21 car. Leonard Wood is famous in the racing world for his innovations; among other things he is credited with inventing the organized, high-speed pit stop.

The Wood brothers were always friendly to me at the track. They were grandfather types, smiling and waving, "Hey! Come over and grab a sandwich." But despite my numerous invitations, they wouldn't come on the show. They'd say, "Oh, we don't like that type of show," meaning, they didn't like not knowing who was calling and what their agenda might be.

Finally, after fifteen years of being asked, Leonard Wood agreed to be a guest on the program. Somehow I finally convinced him that it was safe. I wasn't setting him up, and I had no intention of throwing him under the bus. If something controversial came up, I was going to jump in and handle it. I would never leave him floundering out there! So he came on the air, and it was an absolute dream. It was one of the finest radio shows I've ever done in my life.

For the first fifteen years of hosting *NASCAR Live!*, I'd get up early every Tuesday morning and fly to Daytona Beach, Florida, where the MRN studio was located. I'd do the show that evening and fly back home that same night, which often was a feat unto itself.

In Daytona, the airport is located right next to Daytona International Speedway. The runway literally parallels the backstretch! For much of the time I did the show, we originated from the racetrack, so the second I got off the air, I'd take off my headset, grab my attaché case, run out the door, and jump into a car, where a staffer was waiting for me with the motor running.

Then we'd drive out onto the racetrack heading from Turn Four toward Turn Three in the reverse direction, shoot across the backstretch, and go through the crossover gate. Upon arriving at the airport, I'd run directly to my gate and jump on my Eastern Airlines flight to Birmingham just as the doors were shutting.

After several years of this routine, the airport crew got to know me and would basically just wave me through. Sometimes, they were even kind enough to hold the plane for me. Incredibly, though, they didn't have to do that very often. And when they did, it was usually just for a few seconds.

I got off the air at 7:58:50, and even though the flight departed at 8:03, I made it almost every time.

Much to my disappointment, Eastern eventually eliminated that flight, and for six years or so, I had to spend every Tuesday night in Daytona. Not that I mind Daytona, but since I was on the road constantly, I longed to be at home.

Then everything changed. In the mid '90s, ISDN digital audio service was coming into use, which made it possible for me (and every other radio talk show host) to originate a show from a studio installed in one's home. So my days of traveling to Daytona every Tuesday were gone. The company was thrilled—the savings to the travel budget were significant—and ever since, with the exception of special shows we do on the road, I've been doing NASCAR Live! from my home studio, often wearing shorts, a T-shirt, and flip-flops. Now, at 7:58:50 every Tuesday evening, rather than doing the four-hundred-meter dash to a waiting airplane, I walk into the kitchen to see what's for dinner.

Another enormous change was the introduction of cell phones. Before cell phones, guests had to be sitting next to a landline between 7:00 and 8:00 p.m. EST the night of the show. Now, everybody has a cell phone, and it gives the guests much more flexibility and accessibility. It's a good deal easier to get a guy to agree to be on the show if he doesn't have to change his schedule.

I've had guests call from outside a restaurant where they're about to go in and have dinner with the family. Not long ago, I had a driver call from Fenway Park, where listeners could hear the Red Sox game going on in the background. And several times, drivers have called from a fishing boat or even a hunting stand. Ryan Newman has called in from both locations. Although he never shot anything while on the air with us (I'm guessing his talking scared the deer away), he did catch a fish once during the program.

At the beginning of the segment I said, "How are you doing, Ryan?"

He said, "Great. Hang on a second, I'm just getting this fish into the boat . . ."

We could hear the splash of the bass and the other sounds on the boat, which I think is great. I don't mind. I appreciate guys calling in from wherever. After all, Tuesdays are supposed to be their day off.

Like any radio show, we need to be considerate of our sponsors. But since sponsorship is so important to NASCAR drivers, often we need to double our efforts. For instance, Jeff Burton, who was sponsored by AT&T Mobility, was a recent guest. When we have Burton on the program, we must make sure to run Alltel Wireless commercials at a different point in the hour so that everyone gets the most bang for their buck. And, on the off, off, off chance that a driver's cellular reception is poor and, coincidentally, he is sponsored by a cell phone company? Best to not mention it.

Broadcasters often get invited to host special events. A few years back, I was the master of ceremonies at a fund-raiser for Newberry College in Columbia, South Carolina, where I had the opportunity to share the stage with NASCAR drivers Cale Yarborough and Dale Earnhardt Jr.

Back in the '70s, Yarborough became the first driver to win three consecutive series championships. (Jimmie Johnson recently became the second driver to do so.) Yarborough, long retired, was exactly twice Dale Jr.'s age at the time of the fund-raiser and competed against Earnhardt Sr. when he was just starting out. It was interesting to hear their different perspectives on racing.

At one point, I asked Yarborough to tell the story of the time he and Dale Jr. first met. It was back in the early '80s, and both the Earnhardt and the Yarborough families happened to be staying at the same hotel for the Fourth of July race at Daytona. The two families pulled up to the hotel at the same time, and immediately the kids, including a very young Dale Jr., piled out of their respective cars and made beelines for the swimming pool, while the adults took care of the luggage.

A few moments later, Earnhardt, Yarborough, and their wives were checking in at the front desk when a stern-looking manager came out and said, "Mr. Earnhardt? May I speak with you?"

Earnhardt looked at Yarborough and said, "What could have happened? We've only been here three minutes!"

The manager said, "Mr. Earnhardt, your son is tinkling in the swimming pool."

Earnhardt laughed and said, "Sir, there are thirty kids out there. I'll bet that Dale Jr. is not the only one peeing in that pool!"

The manager said, "Yes, but he's the only one doing it from the diving board."

Back in Brooklyn we called it chutzpah. And Dale Jr. had it. Even then.

Over the years I have been fortunate to do many special events with Richard Petty. He earned his title of "The King" due to his multiple championships and the sport's most wins of 200. (The next most prolific race winner is David Pearson with 105.) Upon his retirement, he became, and remains, an amazingly relentless ambassador for the sport. During his Fan Appreciation Tour, which took place throughout his final year as a driver in 1992, I served as the master of ceremonies at many of the events, including a shindig at Disney World, where Petty was the grand marshal of a huge parade. It was a switch to see Petty riding with Goofy in an old jalopy after years of seeing him whiz past me in his signature STP ride.

One year, I was invited to Maui for the Pontiac Master Dealers Convention, which that season had a racing theme. The owners of the top Pontiac dealerships from across the country were rewarded with a trip to this convention. One of the featured meetings was a program with NASCAR drivers Michael Waltrip, Rusty Wallace, and Richard Petty and NHRA Hall of Famer Don "The Snake" Prudhomme. I served as the master of ceremonies.

During our week in Maui, Claudette and I met Richard and Don for a walk on the beach. Claudette, Don, and I were wearing shorts, T-shirts, and ordinary-looking sunglasses. But Richard came to the beach wearing black shorts, a tank top undershirt, a pair of low-cut black boots, a baseball cap, and his trademark pair of wraparound sunglasses.

We proceeded to take our stroll down Kaanapali Beach, and as we walked, people on their beach towels and in their lounge chairs turned to look. "That looks like Richard Petty. But it can't be."

Finally someone came up and asked him if he was Richard Petty; and when he said yes, the King was immediately besieged by autograph seekers, as he is everywhere he goes. He graciously signed for everyone on anything that was put before him—from coolers to bikini bottoms to hats.

I've never seen Richard turn down a request for an autograph. But I never realized until that day that it wasn't always just a simple paper-and-pen exchange. He was once asked by a reporter, "What's the craziest thing a fan ever asked you to sign?" Without missing a beat, Petty grinned and replied, "A duck."

I wonder who it was that asked him to sign that? Could have been a doctor. Or maybe just some quack.

(Sorry. I couldn't resist.)

NASCAR fans are the most loyal fans in all of sports. When they latch on to a favorite driver and that driver's sponsor, you can bet they won't let go.

The fans also feel a great affinity for the broadcasters. I've always found this incredibly endearing, and I'm flattered when a fan comes up and asks me for an autograph, even if the request is a little unusual. Once, a race fan came out to the stadium in Starkville, Mississippi, where I was doing a University of Alabama football game. He was carrying a large Goodyear racing tire and asked me to sign it. The guy couldn't care less about the ball game. He was a NASCAR fan!

I've come to think the fans feel as if they know me. Sometimes a little too well. Once, in Martinsville, a fan came up to the booth where we were getting ready for the broadcast and knocked on the door. My assistant, Martha, opened the door, and the lady came inside. She was out of breath and excited. "Mr. Eli!" she said. "I'm so happy to meet you. My husband wanted to be here but couldn't. I'm wondering if you could say hello to him on the air? He's never missed a race. He would have been here for sure, only he's bleeding from the rectum."

It was one of maybe three times in my life I truly, truly did not know what to say.

NASCAR people always say that the racing community is like one big family. More than in any other sport, this is true. In basketball or hockey, you're close with your teammates, but you play a different team each game. In NASCAR, the same people compete against each other every week. So drivers and their families really get to know each other.

The same holds true for broadcasters. We get to know each other, the drivers, and all the folks involved with NASCAR. I was always amazed how much people who worked together treated each other like family. This started at the top and worked its way down.

When I started working for MRN, Bill France Jr. was several years into his tenure as NASCAR's chairman, the position he held for thirty-one years. His father, Bill France Sr., aka "Big Bill," is known as the father of stock car racing, a title he richly deserves. One of the most vivid and poignant memories I have of Bill France Sr. is how he used to sit on a cinder block outside our broadcast booth window at Talladega, watching the race. Here he sat on a cinder block at the racetrack he "built"!

As much as his father basically established the sport, it is Bill France Jr. who is largely credited with ushering NASCAR into the mainstream, multibillion-dollar industry it became.

One thing I admired about Bill France Jr. was the fact that he knew his business backward, forward, and sideways. As the story goes, when his father was "building" Daytona International Speedway in the late 1950s, Bill Jr. helped with all aspects of the project, from helping grade the land on what would become the backstretch to cleaning port-a-johns. Coming up in the business, he did every job you could possibly do, from corner worker (one of those guys in the white suits responsible for safety and other issues in a designated area of the track), to flagman (whose job is to signal the drivers), to chief steward (who basically oversees a particular event). When he took over the top job, he knew his stuff and had already earned people's respect.

People described Bill France Jr. as a benevolent dictator. I found him to be incredibly approachable. He was a frequent guest on *NASCAR Live!,* and I always felt he was someone I could go to with a question and get a straight answer, on or off the air.

In February 1990 I was in Daytona for Speed Weeks, which had just gotten underway. I was mildly distracted because my wife, Claudette, who was back in Birmingham, was pregnant and due any day. This was a couple of years before I had a cell phone, so I rented a pager in order for Claudette to reach me the minute she went into labor.

One afternoon I ran into Bill France Jr., who asked, "Hey, when is your wife going to have that baby?"

I said, "As a matter of fact, Mr. France, I'm wearing a pager. The minute she beeps me, I'm heading to the airport to catch the next flight home."

He said, "The heck you are!"

Thinking he wasn't happy about me abandoning my duties, I said, "Excuse me?"

Then he said, "When she calls, you call this number . . ."

The number was for Bruce Alter, who was then NASCAR's chief pilot. Mr. France said I could call the pilot at any time of the day or night, and he would meet me and fly me home to Birmingham in NASCAR's jet.

I said, "That is so generous, sir, but I'll never be able to repay you for that."

He said, "Did you hear me say there was a price attached? The plane is at your disposal. God bless."

A couple of days later, I was doing the broadcast for the Rolex 24, the twenty-four-hour endurance race. I had gotten off the air at midnight and was back at the hotel, getting some sleep before I was due back on the air at 8:00 a.m. But I wouldn't make it for the morning update, because at 5:30 a.m., Claudette called and woke me up. "It's time."

I called Bruce Alter; then I called my boss, John McMullin, so he could put our backup plan in motion and cover me for the broadcast. I quickly showered and shaved and went to the Daytona Beach airport. Bruce Alter and November 500 Romeo, NASCAR'S big Westwind jet, were waiting on me. We flew to Birmingham, and I drove to the hospital, arriving just twenty minutes after Claudette and her aunt Stella had arrived from across town!

As it turned out, my beautiful daughter, Elise, wasn't born until 8:30 that evening. Despite the speed and efficiency of my return home, we—Claudette especially—had a very long day.

To kill the time, I watched the televised race that I had been scheduled to do on the radio that day. Then I turned on the Pro Bowl, which was being played at Aloha Stadium in Hawaii. The game was still on the TV when the doctor came into the room to deliver the baby. He said, "OK, Claudette, we're going to have to ask you to start pushing soon . . ."

At that point, the play-by-play announcer on the Pro Bowl telecast yelled, "What a spectacular catch!"

Instinctively, the doctor, the nurses, and I all turned to watch the replay.

For a brief moment Claudette stopped what she was doing, propped herself up on her elbows, and said, "Excuse me! I'm trying to have a baby here!"

What can I say? It *was* a spectacular catch!

A guy could get used to flying on the NASCAR jet, but most days I was satisfied with commercial airline travel. One Wednesday morning I was sitting on the airplane in Daytona, waiting to fly home after doing *NASCAR Live!* the night before.

Having once again been upgraded to first class, thanks to my frequent flier status, I was comfortably settled into my favorite seat in the first row. They were about to close the door, when I looked out the window and saw three men sprinting across the tarmac. It was Jim Foster, a senior VP for NASCAR; Jim Hunter, NASCAR's VP of Corporate Communications; and Bill France Jr.

As they ran up the stairs and boarded the airplane, I wondered, *Why aren't they on the NASCAR jet?* Maybe some other guy's wife was having a baby? Anyway, I couldn't help but feel a bit self-conscious sitting in first class. So I put the newspaper up in front of my face, hoping I would go unnoticed. But no such luck.

The aisle was clogged with people stowing their carry-on luggage, and Mr. France ended up standing right in front of me. He took his finger, pushed my newspaper down, and said, "We must be paying you too much."

ELEVEN

Talking About Turning Left

A FEW YEARS AFTER LEARNING THE RACING ROPES AT MRN AS A turn announcer, who broadcasts from a tower positioned at one of the turns on the track, and a pit reporter, who broadcasts from pit road, I moved into the booth to co-anchor races with Barney Hall. Barney is *the* radio broadcaster in NASCAR. He is Pat Summerall, Marv Albert, Dick Enberg, Jim Nantz, and Bob Costas all rolled into one.

Barney started his radio career back in 1958 as a disc jockey for WIFM, a station in his hometown of Elkin, North Carolina. He soon branched out into local sports, and according to Barney, when the promoters sent him a bunch of free tickets, he started attending races. He figured as long as he was there, he might as well interview some drivers for his radio show. Next, he was offered the job as PA announcer at the speedway in Bristol, Tennessee, which was brand-new at the time. This led to working for the Daytona 500 network, which initially, in the early '60s, consisted of just three stations in Florida: Daytona, Orlando, and Jacksonville.

By 1970 he was working for MRN, where he has been ever since.

Barney is a wonderful broadcaster, a soothing voice in an otherwise noisy sport. Plus, he probably has the most remarkable sense of humor I've ever encountered. The guy has a line for everything.

One season, Greg Sacks was driving a car for Slim-Fast, the weight-loss shake, and the marketing guys thought it would be a great idea for me to go on the fourteen-day Slim-Fast plan and update the listeners about my progress. Well, I didn't do very well. I don't think I lost any weight. In fact, I may have gained a pound or two. Anyway, Barney had a ball with this.

We were doing a live commercial for Slim-Fast when Barney said, "Well, son, how much weight have you lost?" I hemmed and hawed. Then Barney said, "Folks, this boy's been on the diet for two weeks and all he's lost is fourteen days."

Classic Barney. We could do the best race broadcast of our lives and afterward all anyone would talk about was, "Did you hear that thing Barney said?"

Barney got the best of me many times—on and off the air. A few days after my daughter, Elise, was born, I flew from my home in Birmingham back to Daytona for Speed Weeks, which was underway. When I got to the track, being the proud papa that I was, I immediately went into the garage to hand out cigars. But every time I stopped to hand someone a cigar, I'd hear, "Oh, no thanks. Barney already gave me a cigar. He just had a daughter."

He'd gone around ahead of me and given out dozens of cigars. To this day—over nineteen years after he stole my thunder—when I see Barney, I ask him, "How's your daughter? She looks more and more like you every day."

I never minded Barney's ribbing, because the guy doesn't have a mean bone in his body. Listeners could tell that our on-air banter was all in good fun. As Barney always says, "If we're having fun, the listeners are having fun."

I took that to heart along with his other advice. Probably the most important thing Barney taught me was to slow down. Early on he told me, "Just because the cars are going two hundred miles per hour doesn't mean you have to!"

He also helped me learn how to make the most of our full crew. This was new to me; in the minor leagues of hockey and baseball, I had always worked as a one-man band. Now, during MRN broadcasts we had two anchorpeople, two or three turn people, and three or four pit people all passing the proverbial baton back and forth. Barney or our producer, John McMullin, would say, "Don't forget to go to Ned. He's got a crew chief standing by . . ."

Barney also showed me how to keep track of things like pit stops and lead changes. I'd always look over to see what notes Barney was scribbling. And luckily for me, I had a lot of help keeping track of positions and rundowns. I had Martha Oliver by my side.

When I first met Martha, her name was Martha Mew, so we affectionately called her "that little Mew girl." Later, she became Martha Oliver when she married David Oliver, a man well known in racing circles, whose résumé includes everything from jack man for Richard Petty to shop foreman for Roush Racing.

Basically, Martha was our statistical whiz in the booth. She did all the scoring so we'd know who was running at what position. This was before we had computers. In the early days Martha kept score with a pen and yellow legal paper! She kept a chart for every lap and wrote the numbers down as the drivers came around. When a driver got lapped, she circled the number. Then, when I needed the information, she'd hand me notes or point things out to me. She was another pair of eyes and became another part of my brain. Martha and I were so different and had such different backgrounds that it's amazing we got along so well together. Or maybe that's why we got along. I came to depend on her in the booth as well as on the road.

One weekend, we had a race in Dover, Delaware. Martha and the crew arrived there ahead of me. I was due to arrive at the Philadelphia airport at three in the morning. Since the rental car office would be closed at that hour, I had asked Martha to pick up a car and leave it for me so I could drive to Dover when I landed. She agreed, and per our plan, she was to park the car in an accessible spot, hide the key on top of the right rear tire, and put a note on the front seat confirming that this was my vehicle. Then, she was to leave me a voice mail regarding the car's location.

I landed and checked my messages, "Eli, the car is under the fir tree . . ."

Despite the late hour, I had to call Martha. "So sorry to wake you, Martha. But I'm from Brooklyn. We only had one tree in Brooklyn. I wouldn't know a fir tree from a fur coat. This is a huge parking lot with a bunch of cars and a bunch of trees. A little help?"

Martha said, "Eli, I'm from South Carolina, and we had lots of trees. Just walk out the front door, look for the first car wedged under something that looks like a Christmas tree, with a note on the front seat that says 'ELI' in big block letters. That would be the one."

Working for MRN over the years, I had the opportunity to interview all the great champions of racing. But often we would get the chance to interview people outside the sport as well. We just never knew who might show up in our broadcast booth.

One year, a gentleman by the name of Terry Bollea was invited to be the grand marshal at the Daytona 500. Terry is better known by his stage name, Hulk Hogan. A few laps into the race, he walked into the booth. We were still doing the play-by-play, so he came in and sat inconspicuously in the back. Well, as inconspicuously as he could, being a six-foot-seven, 302-pound man wearing red spandex tights, a ripped shirt, and a yellow feather boa.

When the turn guys started talking, he came over and politely extended his hand, "Eli? Barney? I'm Terry Bollea. It's a great pleasure to meet you. I've listened to you guys for years. I love NASCAR. I was a big Richard Petty fan growing up in Tampa . . ."

The producer gave him a headset, then Barney and I started talking again. "Dale Earnhardt continues to lead, and joining us in the booth is the legendary Hulk Hogan . . ."

"Eli, when I was a young Hulkster, I used to watch Richard Petty . . ." Immediately, he became a different guy. Completely in character. He slapped me on the arm just hard enough so the slap could be heard on the radio. "Man, you've got some guns on ya!"

Everyone in the press box, which was just through the glass, was laughing and standing up to get a better view. Then he pointed to Barney, who probably weighs fifty pounds soaking wet. "Who's this little guy here? Is that your manager?"

A hilarious and great interview. Then, we were back to the race, "OK, thanks, Hulk. Everybody, that was Hulk Hogan, in town to drop the flag for us today. The leader is still Dale Earnhardt in Turn One . . ."

Immediately, in the booth we had Terry Bollea back again. Polite, calm, and respectful. He shook our hands, got up, and exited quietly. Again, as quietly as a person can while standing over six and a half feet tall and wearing head-to-toe neon red and yellow.

A less flamboyant but no less interesting guest was Oliver North, the retired marine colonel who came to fame in the 1980s during the Iran-Contra scandal. North joined us in Richmond, where at the time he was running for the Senate as the Republican candidate from Virginia.

Richmond is a short track, so when the play-by-play announcer stops talking, the guy in the turn talks; then eight seconds later it's your turn to talk again. So it's tough to weave in long questions with detailed answers. But I wasn't going to break new ground on illegal arms sales. We kept it light.

The amazing thing was, no matter what topic we discussed, North would somehow personally connect it to Barney or me. If I'd mention the short track, he'd say, "Well, Eli, you're lucky. You live in Birmingham, so you've got short tracks down there." He knew that Barney owned a golf course. He knew that I grew up in New York. Obviously, he'd been briefed. He was slick.

After he left the booth, Barney leaned over to me and said off the air, "Son, there's your first exposure to big-time politics."

We had other political guests over the years. There was a governor from a Northeastern state who tried to be as smooth as Oliver North but unfortunately kept calling me "Barney" and kept addressing Barney as "Eli." We interviewed Vice President Dan Quayle not long after he made his famous gaffe of misspelling *potato* during a visit to an elementary school. We had a lot of fun torturing our producer by saying we intended to ask the vice president to spell *broccoli*. But we never did.

Another gentleman I met at a racetrack and later had the opportunity to sit next to at a banquet was Supreme Court Justice Clarence Thomas. He was funny, gregarious, and—as I was surprised to learn—a huge racing fan. This man didn't just follow NASCAR; he owned a motor home and went to races. He not only knew who Kevin Harvick was; he knew that Harvick's wife's name was DeLana and that her family, the Linvilles, were from Kernersville, North Carolina. He really knew his stuff.

Back in 1984, President Ronald Reagan made history when he became the first sitting U.S. president to attend a NASCAR race. The occasion was the Firecracker 400 at Daytona and Richard Petty's two hundredth win—and on the Fourth of July no less. I'll never forget the majestic sight of Air Force One landing at Daytona International Airport, where the runway parallels the backstretch of the speedway. The two are so close that even your average Sunday golfer could hit a ball from one to the other, although the Secret Service would have frowned on anyone doing it that day.

Reagan stayed for the entire event and congratulated Petty in Victory Lane. So I guess you could say the president congratulated the King. (Sorry, I couldn't help myself.) He also attended a private postrace concert and joined NASCAR drivers, families, crew, and members of the media to hear Tammy Wynette sing "Stand by Your Man."

The honor of interviewing the president for our broadcast fell to Ned Jarrett, who did a wonderful job.

As a driver, Ned Jarrett was a big winner. He later admitted that he retired from racing far too early, but at least he knew that after retirement he wanted to become a broadcaster. Before he signed on with MRN, he even put himself through the Dale Carnegie course to improve his public-speaking skills. He didn't want to erase his North Carolina roots, but he wanted to polish his image and speak with more confidence.

He became great at his job partly due to the fact that he was so well liked. If you didn't like Ned, there was something wrong with you. Everyone called him "Gentleman Ned Jarrett," due to his good manners and calm demeanor. This carried him a long way in broadcasting.

In addition to his popularity and his knowledge of the business, Ned succeeded because he was good on his feet. During a race at Martinsville, Ned was our pit reporter, who also had the responsibility of interviewing the winner in Victory Lane. So, with approximately twenty-five laps to go, Ned excused himself to go to the restroom. During a commercial break he told everybody, "Hey, I'm making a quick pit stop before I go to Victory Lane, so don't come to me for a while."

The restroom at Martinsville is very close to pit road, so Ned should have been in and out in no time. But the moment he reached the men's room there was a loud commotion on the track. Richard

Petty had run over some piece of debris that cut his tire and forced him to immediately wrestle his car down to pit road.

At that moment, I believe it was Mike Joy who said on the air, "There's trouble with Richard Petty . . ." Then, forgetting Ned's whereabouts, he instinctively said, "Let's go to Ned Jarrett on pit road."

Having been around racing for so long, Ned knew the sounds going on just outside the restroom door. He heard the car coming down pit road and stopping. He heard the air impact wrench loosening the lug nuts. He heard the sound of the new tire and lug nuts being put on. He heard the car being dropped off the jack and speeding away. And being a good broadcaster, he was able to describe it all without even seeing it. In fact, he described the whole scene while standing right in front of the urinal. The folks at home and, at first, most of his fellow broadcasters had no idea that two-time Grand National Champion Ned Jarrett had just done a beautiful, spot-on pit report from inside the men's room at Martinsville Speedway.

As much fun as we had, and as much as we laughed on the NASCAR beat, our crew knew when it was time to get serious. Unfortunately, there have been many, many somber occasions over the years.

Accidents, injuries, and fatalities are a regrettable part of racing. Drivers put their lives on the line during every practice and every race. Sadly, racing has seen more than its fair share of tragedies, both on and off the track.

In April 1993, just prior to the race at Bristol, 1992 Winston Cup Champion Alan Kulwicki died in a plane crash. He was returning from a public appearance in Knoxville when the small plane on which he was a passenger went down just prior to its approach into the Tri-Cities Regional Airport near Blountville, Tennessee.

The following day (a cold, nasty day in Bristol) Kulwicki's truck, this giant eighteen-wheeled transporter, pulled out onto the racetrack as drivers, crew members, and media people watched. The truck, which had a black wreath affixed to its grille, drove a slow lap around the track, then exited out the crossover gate and started down the road back toward Charlotte, where Kulwicki's shop was located. I learned that day what it was like to see dozens of grown men, myself included, stand in the rain and cry.

In July of that same year, the NASCAR community suffered another huge loss when Davey Allison died following a helicopter crash at the Talladega Super Speedway. I was at home in Birmingham when I heard the news.

Just one day earlier, I had flown home with Davey on his plane following the New Hampshire race. Davey and his father, Bobby, often gave me a lift when they had extra room. On this trip, we flew from New Hampshire to Charlotte, where we dropped off Davey's crew chief, Larry McReynolds, and car owner, Robert Yates. Then we flew to Alabama.

During the flight, Davey mentioned that David Bonnett, Neil Bonnett's son, was going to be testing a race car in Talladega the next day. "If I get time, I'm going to take the helicopter over and watch him," he said. That's how it was with the Alabama Gang. Everybody was like family.

The next day, I was in the house and heard one of those quick TV news bulletins: "A helicopter has gone down at the Talladega Race Track . . ."

I got really cold. I turned to my wife and said, "That's Davey."

She said, "What?"

I said, "That's Davey."

Who else would have been attempting to land a helicopter at the track in Talladega? It was closed that day except for David Bonnett's test run.

Sadly, it turned out to be true. Davey, along with his passenger, Red Farmer, had flown to Talladega. Davey was attempting to land inside a fenced-in area of the track's infield when the nose of the helicopter flipped up suddenly, causing it to crash. Neil Bonnett, who was at the track, actually pulled Red Farmer from the wreckage but was unable to reach Davey. Paramedics freed Davey and rushed him and Farmer to the hospital. Farmer recovered from his injuries, but Davey, who had suffered major head trauma, died the next day.

The weekend after Davey's death, there was an empty space in the garage at the Pocono Raceway where his truck would have normally been parked. It was empty except for a huge wreath, which made for a heart-wrenching sight. Dale Earnhardt won the race, and when he drove out to the start-finish line, a crew member handed him a Davey Allison flag. Earnhardt held it up outside his window and took a victory lap with the flag flying. What a tribute!

Barney and I were watching from the booth and were so choked up that neither of us could speak, which is not very good on radio! Our producer was gesturing to us and saying (in our ears), "Somebody say something!"

But we couldn't talk without crying on the air. So the producer switched to another circuit and said to the guys on pit road, "For crying out loud! Somebody say something!"

Jim Phillips, our lead pit reporter, jumped in and was able to carry the broadcast until we regained our composure.

Less than a year after Davey Allison died, NASCAR lost one of its most popular drivers, and sadly, the Alabama Gang lost another member, when Neil Bonnett was killed.

During his eighteen-year career, Bonnett won eighteen series races. His highest finish in the points chase was in 1985, when he finished fourth, the same year his teammate, Darrell Waltrip, won the championship.

In 1990 Bonnett was seriously injured in a crash at Darlington and retired from racing. He recovered and soon began a career in broadcasting, where among other things he hosted his own TV show, *Neil Bonnett's Winners* on TNN. He was incredibly good at it. He had the talent to teach people about racing. He could make even the most technical stuff understandable to the folks at home. As good as he was on the air, though, Neil never lost the itch to go back to racing. Everybody told him, "Neil, you have nothing to prove!"

But how can anybody tell a guy to not pursue his dream? He missed racing too much, and by 1993 he was competing again.

Then came the start of the 1994 season. During an afternoon practice session before the very first race, the Daytona 500, Bonnett's car hit the outside wall nearly head-on. When the crash occurred, I was in the MRN booth, editing some interviews I had done earlier in the week to use during our broadcast. Barney Hall was a couple of booths down from me, doing the public address announcing, which in those days, MRN used to do at almost all the tracks. I didn't see the impact, but I heard Barney say over the loudspeaker that there was a problem, so I walked over to ask what was going on.

Barney said, "Man, the car just shot up into the wall."

It was a sickening feeling. It wasn't long before we learned that Neil had died on impact.

Neil Bonnett was an original. He was a fantastic person to be around, and I got to know him very well. We

Hosting the pre-race activities at Daytona International Speedway did some work together on the air, and we often traveled together when we flew home with fellow Alabama Gang members Bobby and Davey Allison on their planes.

Many of us flew to Bonnett's home in Hueytown, Alabama, for the memorial service. Since Speed Weeks was underway, there was also a service in Daytona. A dark cloud hung over the race that year. Perhaps Buddy Baker put it best: "When I get to heaven, I'm going to kill Neil Bonnett."

I'm sad to say that I've witnessed several fatalities and more terrible accidents than I can count. Often, you see something on the track that looks so bad you can't believe the driver could possibly survive. Back in 1984, during the Busch Clash (now the Budweiser Shootout) at Speed Weeks in Daytona, Ricky Rudd, who was driving for Bud Moore in the Wrangler car, got a nudge coming off Turn Four. Suddenly the car went sideways and began barrel-rolling and spinning on its nose, with pieces of the car flying off, before it finally landed on the grass. No one on our crew had ever seen such a savage-looking accident. We were sure we had just seen a man lose his life. Incredibly, though, Rudd was fine, minus some pretty major bumps and bruises. He was back competing the next week at Richmond, although he had to actually tape his swollen eyelids open so he could see well enough to drive.

Perhaps the most mind-blowing thing I've seen on a racetrack was Michael Waltrip's 1990 wreck during the Busch race at Bristol, when he came off Turn Two and hit the wall. Upon impact, his car virtually disintegrated. It looked like a Beirut car bombing. It was absolutely unbelievable. When the remnants of the car came to a stop, the track became deathly quiet. There was a complete hush over the crowd. Immediately, members of the safety crew ran toward the carnage.

Michael's brother, Darrell, who was understandably beside himself, also ran out to the scene.

When they reached the car, the crew guys pulled away what used to be the bodywork of Waltrip's Pontiac. I mean, it was basically gone. Nothing but a bent roll cage. Then, incredibly, Michael Waltrip stepped out, dusted himself off, and hopped on a golf cart to proceed to the infield care center.

How he didn't lose his legs, let alone his life, is a tribute to NASCAR's safety standards. I truly could not believe what I was seeing. When something like this happens—or should I say when there is an accident, because nothing like this had ever happened—you have to be very careful what you say on the air.

With Dale Earnhardt driving, this car about "took me out" at Pocono Int'l Raceway in 1982. The sheet metal that's missing from the car is now in my office in Birmingham.

Broadcasters cannot speculate. I was trained by people at MRN and NASCAR to simply describe what I see. This extends to other sports as well. If a player is injured on the football field, you're safe in detailing only what you know for certain. I'm not a doctor. I never say, "I bet he's got a broken collarbone." I only say, "He's getting up and walking off the field. Apparently, he's favoring one side."

In NASCAR it's even more important to not speculate. And even when you've confirmed the worst, broadcasters still hold back. When Neil Bonnett died, we knew it but couldn't say anything on the air until NASCAR was able to reach his family. This was before cell phones were common, and tragically, his wife, Susan, was in the car, driving from Alabama to Daytona, and couldn't be reached.

I'm sad to say that somebody leaked the information that Bonnett had died, and Susan heard the news on the radio. I can only imagine how that added to her pain.

Over the years I've often been asked if race car drivers have a death wish. I understand the reason for the question. But my answer is no. I genuinely believe that NASCAR drivers are master competitors. They accept the dangers of their sport but are compelled to compete at the highest level. The perfect example of this is the late Dale Earnhardt.

On February 18, 2001, I was working Turn Four at the Daytona 500 at Daytona International Speedway.

To NASCAR drivers, a Daytona 500 win is arguably the most coveted racing prize. Ironically, despite all his championships and all his wins, it wasn't until 1998 that Dale Earnhardt finally won the Great American Race. Three years later, Earnhardt was as determined as ever to visit this particular Victory Lane yet again.

As the 2001 race got underway, Earnhardt's trademark Number 3 black Chevrolet led for several laps early on. Then, at lap 174 he dodged a huge eighteen-car pile-up that left others, including Tony Stewart, tumbling by the wayside. By the end of the race, Earnhardt's teammates, Michael Waltrip and Dale Earnhardt Jr., were battling for the lead while he was running third, going three wide, with Sterling Marlin to his left and Kenny Schrader to his right.

Then, on the very last lap of the race, while Earnhardt was protecting his teammates' lead, Marlin's and Earnhardt's cars made contact. Earnhardt's car turned sharply up the track, collided with Schrader, and hit the wall nose first.

I was on the air for this entire sequence. My attention had been on the battle for the lead, which at that point was coming out of Turn Four. I was talking about Waltrip and Dale Jr. when I said, "Meanwhile, from third on back, things are backing up. Dale Earnhardt has gone into the wall . . ."

I then handed it off to the anchor guys in the booth for the conclusion of the race, which Waltrip won. In the meantime, Earnhardt's car had come to a rolling stop, virtually in front of me.

The accident didn't look severe. It looked routine, if there is such a thing as a routine accident at 185 miles per hour. Certainly, Earnhardt had been in dozens of similar wrecks, and I had seen many exactly like this over the years. But right away, I knew something was wrong when I saw Kenny Schrader walk up to Earnhardt's car, look inside, and start waving frantically for the safety crew.

I picked up my binoculars and looked into the car. I couldn't tell anything except that there was no movement. That was unusual because normally when a driver comes to a stop, he often begins to unhook his safety gear and immediately brings the window net down. This is a universal sign in NASCAR that the driver is OK. But Earnhardt's window net was still up.

I had a sick feeling, but I suspected, I hoped, that Dale had just been knocked out. The broadcast ended without us knowing for sure. We later learned that he had died instantly when his car hit the wall.

The great Dale Earnhardt was dead at age forty-nine.

To the NASCAR world, losing Dale Earnhardt was unimaginable.

Along with Richard Petty, he was stock car racing's biggest star, beloved by fans as the scrappy workingman's competitor. But as the unprecedented media coverage of his death proved, his popularity stretched far beyond the racing world. His death was at the top of every Sunday night newscast and on the front page of every Monday morning newspaper. His funeral was televised live on multiple TV networks, including CNN and the Fox News Channel. Fans flocked by the thousands to mourn him at several sites, including the Daytona track and his headquarters in Mooresville, North Carolina. A make-shift shrine even popped up at GM World Headquarters in Detroit.

Hosting a NASCAR press conference at the Starlight Roof at New York's Waldorf=Astoria Hotel with Dale Earnhardt (L) and NASCAR Chairman Bill France, Jr. (at podium)

If something positive came out of this tragedy, it was all the safety improvements that have been implemented following Earnhardt's death. NASCAR now mandates the use of head and neck restraints and other innovations, such as safer barriers and the soft wall concept, that will benefit drivers for years to come.

There's no question that NASCAR has forged on with great young stars such as Jeff Gordon, Tony Stewart, Jimmie Johnson, and, of course, Dale Jr. But Earnhardt is still deeply, deeply missed. There was just no one like him. He won seven championships, but even when he didn't win, he was spinning and grinning and intimidating. He was the Man in Black.

It's hard for people who knew him only as the Intimidator to imagine this, but the guy had a heart of gold.

Once, I got a phone call from a dad in Alabama whose son was terminally ill. He introduced himself and told me that his son was dying, and all the boy wanted in the world was to talk to Dale Earnhardt.

Well, I called Dale. I got him on the phone while he was out riding on his tractor! I explained the situation. I also told him that I didn't know these folks and that I knew he got requests like this all the time, but if I could just give him their number, then I would leave it up to him.

A few days later the dad called me and said, "You won't believe this! Dale called and must have spent thirty minutes on the phone with my son. We were uncomfortable keeping him so long, but he wouldn't get off the phone!"

The day after the phone call, a big box arrived at the boy's house, full of all sorts of hats, T-shirts, and other Earnhardt memorabilia. The dad wanted me to know that Dale had done all this.

The next week, I saw Dale at the racetrack in Richmond and told him that the dad had called and told me what he did. I started to say, "That was very, very kind of you," but Dale interrupted me.

"OK," he said, "but don't let me hear a word about it on the air. I didn't do that for publicity. I just did it. So promise me you won't put that story on the air."

I never told the story until he passed away. That was the Dale Earnhardt a lot of us were lucky enough to know.

Preparing to call the turn action at Talladega with security in place

Butch Owens (L) and Martha Oliver (R) with me at the New Hampshire Motor Speedway. Without these two dear friends and co-workers, I would never have enjoyed the successes that I have.

Touchdown Alabama . . . Touchdown Auburn . . . With my dear friend, the late Jim Fyffe, the long-time "voice" of the Auburn Tigers

Larry McReynolds (dark blazer) and I close in on air time for a NASCAR Truck Series Race at the Mesa Marin Raceway in Bakersfield, California.

TWELVE

Welcome to Television

TALK ABOUT A SNOW DAY. ON FEBRUARY 18, 1979, SOME OF THE worst weather in the world blanketed the North American continent. All of the Eastern Seaboard and parts of the Midwest were covered in snow and ice. Airports were closed. No one could get in or out. As a result, almost everyone residing in these areas was at home. And many of them were watching TV.

As luck would have it, that particular day marked the first time a NASCAR race was covered live and in its entirety on network television when CBS broadcast the Daytona 500. Previously, races were only televised in part, usually airing after the fact, and more often than not, only as highlights on programs such as ABC's *Wide World of Sports*. Back then, there weren't five hundred stations from which to choose—more like five or six. On that day, millions of viewers were tuned to CBS.

While the rest of the country was socked in, Daytona Beach, Florida, was enjoying spectacular blue skies and sunny weather, which set an ideal scene for the Great American Race. The race was thrilling, especially the finish. Cale Yarborough and Donnie Allison were battling for the lead when they crashed on the backstretch. Richard Petty, who was running a distant third, came around to win the race. But that wasn't the end of it.

While Petty took the checkered flag, Yarborough and Allison climbed out of their cars and got into a fistfight. Meanwhile, Donnie Allison's brother, Bobby, who was also competing in the race, stopped his car where the two were fighting, jumped out, and joined in the brawl. After the fact, Bobby Allison famously said, "I don't understand what happened. Cale's nose just kept hitting my fist."

The combination of captive audience and captivating event pushed the ratings through the roof. NASCAR and network television were officially engaged, and over the next decade or so, this relationship would become a rock-solid marriage.

Many different agreements with several networks would follow that first NASCAR-CBS television contract, which CBS Sports president Neal Pilson and NASCAR chairman Bill France Jr. famously celebrated at one of Mr. France's favorite restaurants, the Steak-n-Shake on Volusia Avenue in Daytona Beach. By the 1989 season, every NASCAR race was being telecast. The following year, The Nashville Network (TNN) joined other networks and began including auto racing in its programming offerings.

A pensive moment just prior to air time of a truck series race in Flemington, NJ

Despite the fact that I was a lifelong radio guy, in 1996 I signed on as the anchorman for TNN's NASCAR coverage. I had serious reservations about moving to television. I had very little TV experience, and—let's be honest—I had gray hair. I was overweight. I'm not your typical

"Ken doll" sort of persona. Plus, the decision was very difficult for me because I didn't want to leave MRN, the network I'd been with for all but six years of its existence. MRN was my home.

But as much as I love radio, this was a promotion for me. TV has more viewers, more sponsors, and more money. Ultimately, I spoke to Bill France Jr. and asked him, "Are you sure this is the right thing for me to do?"

He said, "Would I be leading you down this path if it wasn't right for you? Just listen to me. We need you to go to television."

That was good enough for me. He arranged for me to meet with David Hall, who was the president of TNN and a wonderful guy—a great human being and a genuine friend. So even though I've always said I have a face for radio, I took the plunge and moved to TV.

My first NASCAR telecast for TNN was at Rockingham, North Carolina, the second race of the schedule. (CBS covered the first race at Daytona.) I was a little bit nervous, but I was prepared, and I knew the subject matter. We did our prerace rehearsal on the roof of the press box. Then, since we had about an hour until we went on the air, the crew dispersed. Some people went to get something to eat; a couple of people made a quick trip to the garage; others were in the press box, talking or going over their notes. I, on the other hand, had been waiting all morning to visit the men's room. This was my opportunity, and much to my relief, that's where I headed. No sooner had I settled in when I heard a commotion outside the door. Someone was yelling, "Where's Eli? Anybody seen Eli?"

I thought, *Man, can't a guy get a moment to himself?* Then I yelled back through the bathroom door, "Yeah? What's up?"

"The St. Petersburg satellite just went down," the guy said. "You're on the air in three minutes hosting *Race Day.*"

TNN President David Hall (L) and Director of Motorsports Mark Kuchan (R) announcing my hiring

Race Day was a one-hour magazine show that covered all kinds of motorsports, including drag racing, road course racing, World of Outlaws, and motorcycles. The program preceded our broadcast of the NASCAR race, and that particular day, the host, Rick Benjamin, was doing the show live from St. Petersburg, Florida, which was the site of the IMSA Road Race running later that day. But the satellite went down, and they needed me to take over. Immediately.

For a split second I thought this might be a first-day-on-the-job joke. But I had no time to think, so I buttoned up, washed my hands, grabbed my sport jacket, and charged up to the roof like a wild buffalo. Luckily, I already had makeup on, and my earpiece was in my shirt pocket, so as someone handed me a microphone, I plugged in my wires and assumed my position in front of the camera. Then my producer, Pam Miller, said in my ear, "St. Petersburg is down. We're doing the show. Just follow me."

I was familiar enough with the show to know when to take a

breath and when to start talking, but I had no idea what we were actually doing on the show. The next thing I knew, the music started, Pam was counting me down, and we were on the air.

Fortunately, I knew just enough about other types of motorsports to be dangerous. I kept track, in a cursory manner, of all the different sanctioning bodies, the names of the tracks, and who was racing where. This came in incredibly handy at that moment, because it was time to start talking. "Today on *Race Day* the straight liners are in the desert southwest, the World of Outlaws is running in Nebraska, NASCAR is in Rockingham, and the road course stars are in St. Petersburg . . ."

At that moment I was grateful for all my years in radio. If there's one thing you learn as a radio broadcaster, it's how to ad-lib. I also had Pam Miller's help. When she said, "Pitch to Ron Capps on tape talking about the race in Phoenix in ten, nine, eight, seven . . . ," while she was counting me down, on the air I said, "Why don't we start in Phoenix at Firebird Raceway, where race number two of the NHRA season is about to get underway. Ron Capps is driving for Don 'the Snake' Prudhomme . . ."

On air for TNN at the Heartland Park road course in Topeka, Kansas

All of a sudden, video of Ron Capps appeared from somewhere. I have no idea where the heck from. But it was rolling! We went on this way for about twenty-five minutes, when, thankfully, the satellite issues in St. Petersburg were rectified and I turned it over to Rick Benjamin. "Rick, you guys are going to have quite a day down there . . ."

What a rush. But that's what live television is all about. I then, finally, returned to the bathroom without further incident. Whew!!!

As a radio broadcaster, you don't have to worry about how you look. I mean, a guy should be presentable, but he certainly doesn't have to concern himself with makeup. On TV, you do. We all know what happened to Richard Nixon when he went without makeup during his 1960 presidential debate with John F. Kennedy. (Note to really young people: Nixon looked awful. And he lost.)

Television lights wash you out. If you go on the air without makeup, you'll look like a piece of boiled chicken. One of the funniest scenes I have ever witnessed took place prior to the taping of *The Stock Car Legends Reunion*, a documentary featuring the greatest of NASCAR's old-time stars.

Before we started the show, which I cohosted with Ken Squier, the guests climbed into tall director's chairs that were set up under the lights. You haven't lived until you've seen Buddy Baker and Dave Marcis sitting next to Junior Johnson and Cale Yarborough, all with their eyes closed while talented makeup artists fuss over them, dabbing on concealer and powdering their faces to a matte finish.

Unfortunately, on television you also have to think about your hair. I never worried so much about my own. But during our TNN telecasts, we often had to watch out for renowned crew-chief-turned-broadcaster Larry McReynolds.

One weekend we were preparing for the broadcast of the NASCAR Busch Series race in Hickory, North Carolina. The broadcast booth wasn't spacious enough to facilitate an on-camera stand-up from inside, so we stepped outside for the shot.

Larry is not "follicley" blessed to start with, and what little hair he does have is very, very fine. On this particularly windy day his hair was flying everywhere. With about one minute to airtime, Larry looked as though he had just licked a light socket.

The producer said in my ear, "Geez! Do something with Larry's hair!"

I thought, *Who am I? Vidal Sassoon?*

I looked to my assistant, Martha Oliver. "Martha, do you have any hair spray?"

She said, "Sure."

"Give it to me!" I said.

So I started spraying Larry's hair with generous amounts of Aqua Net Extreme Hold while the producer began counting us down: "Sixty seconds!" I had my microphone under my arm while I patted down his hair. I kept spraying and spraying. Then Martha took over and sprayed some more. With just seconds to spare, we had his hair lacquered down to our satisfaction. In fact, we may have overdone it. He could have sustained hurricane-force winds after our efforts.

Jeff Burton (dark shirt) and his brother Ward (white shirt) are my guests on "This Week In NASCAR"

At the next race, Larry said, "Boy, you guys did a great job last week. My hair didn't move until Wednesday."

In television, you never know what crisis will arise just seconds to airtime.

Just prior to a telecast for an Indy Race in Charlotte, Martha noticed that the window in the booth was filthy. Since there was no way to eliminate the window from the shot, she moved quickly to get it cleaned. In the early days of cable TV, staff was often limited, so Martha went downstairs, found some Windex, and returned to the booth, intending to clean it herself. By the time she got back, Tom Sneeva, my color man for Indy events, was already in position next to me. Space was tight, and Martha couldn't reach the window.

"Here, Eli," she said, handing me the Windex and some paper towels.

So, just a minute or so before anchoring this national telecast, I was wiping bird poop off the broadcast booth window. When you're part of a crew, you do what you have to do.

Technical problems are common, and these days a TV crew would never travel to a track without a backup generator. But once, during my early days with TNN, we did just that. Just prior to a race at the Hickory Speedway, a truck hit an electrical pole on the highway near the racetrack and wiped out all the power in the neighborhood. The track itself was operational; they had battery backups. But we got knocked off the air. We were dead.

The engineers immediately ran an extension cord from one of the track's working electrical outlets, tethered that chord to a bunch of other chords, and ran it all the way out to our satellite truck. Then one of our cameramen, Wayne Womack, using his single camera, started shooting the race from atop the roof of the racetrack. He just followed the leaders.

Meanwhile, I rushed to the satellite truck, where we had a three-inch black-and-white monitor. An audio assistant hastily plugged a handheld microphone into the back of an audio mixer and handed it to me.

I sat on a stool, looked at that tiny TV screen (the same image the folks at home were seeing, except much smaller), and called the race from inside the truck. I couldn't even see the track!

Since we didn't have headsets, the director would call a guy in the truck when it was time for a commercial, and he would signal me by hand. And to allow everybody to keep track of who was running where, Wayne the cameraman would on occasion pan his camera over to the scoreboard so the viewers at home, and I in the satellite truck, would know the lap count and the top five on the leader board.

But for most of the day, all the viewers saw were images of the front few cars, with my voice in the background.

That wasn't the only unusual day at the Hickory Speedway. When I was working for MRN, our race broadcasts at that particular track would on occasion get interrupted by funerals. The Catawba Memorial Gardens Cemetery, where, among others, legendary NASCAR driver Bobby Isaac is buried, is located just outside of Turns One and Two of the racetrack. When a funeral was scheduled for the same time as a race, the race would temporarily stop while the ceremony took place.

The drivers and broadcasters always knew about it ahead of time. At the appointed hour the officials would throw the red flag to stop the event. Cars would stop. The public address announcing would cease. On the air, we'd tell the listeners that we were taking a break for the Johnson family funeral, and we would run features and interviews for fifteen minutes or so to give the family time to bury their loved one. Once the mourners returned to their cars and drove out of the cemetery, the race would resume.

Whether it's live radio or live TV, improvisation is key. During the 2000 race at the New Hampshire International Speedway (now the New Hampshire Motor Speedway), the grand marshal was

Former driver and current broadcaster Phil Parsons (R) joins me on the track to tape a segment for a TNN telecast.

baseball great Ted Williams. As a lifelong Yankees fan, I typically had no use for the Red Sox, but for Williams I made an exception. The hitting champion and Hall of Famer known as Teddy Ballgame and the Splendid Splinter was one of the best of all time.

After fulfilling his prerace duties— "Gentlemen, start your engines!"— Williams came up to the booth to join us for an interview.

By 2000 Williams was an older man and in poor health. He often used a wheelchair and needed assistance getting around. When he came into our booth, I was on the air, but I watched out of the corner of my eye as someone helped him down the stairs and positioned him on a stool against the wall.

I was instructed that during the next commercial I should walk over to the wall at the end of the long, narrow booth where Williams sat, and I would be handed a stick microphone to conduct our interview. When the commercial started, I moved into position next to him, and we exchanged pleasantries.

Then, while the commercial ran—it was a long one—Williams started to lean forward. I mean, really far forward, as if he was keeling over. So producer Pam Miller said into my ear, "What's going on?"

I didn't want to embarrass Williams by answering her out loud, and besides, I didn't know what was going on. All I knew was that by this point, he was listing at a very awkward angle, looking at the floor. So I looked into the camera, knowing Pam would be watching, and just shrugged.

"Do something!" she said.

Of course our viewers were not privy to any of this, since we were still in commercial. Then I heard the executive producer Patti Wheeler in my ear: "Do something! Anything!"

I switched the microphone from my left to my right hand, and with my left hand, which is my dominant hand and was closest to Williams, I grabbed the back of his collar and pulled him straight up. It was somewhat unwieldy because I had to hold him while reaching across my body with the microphone. Nonetheless, I conducted the interview, all the while holding the Splendid Splinter by the scruff of his neck. He was fantastic, a superb interview. And it looked to all of America as if old Eli, a Yankees fan, had his arm around Ted Williams. Like we were the best of buddies.

Once at that same track, Donald Trump was in the crowd. We didn't get the opportunity to interview him, but at one point during a commercial break, our cameraman spotted him walking through the garage with his entourage and put him on the screen. I was in the booth with former-champion-turned-colorman Buddy Baker and Dr. Dick Berggren, my fellow broadcaster, who would later become the lead pit reporter for Fox Sports.

When we came out of the break, I said, "Welcome back to New Hampshire International Speedway. Look who's here today. It's . . . the Donald! And for those of you just tuning in, I'm the Eli, he's the Buddy, and he's . . ."

I paused for a split second, looked at Dick Berggren, and realized what I was about to say. Instead, I said, ". . . and he's the . . . Dr. Dick Berggren."

Through my earpiece I could hear peals of laughter from the guys and girls in the production truck. It's amazing what the human brain can do when it really has to.

Working for TNN led to the opportunity to do the play-by-play for several CBS telecasts. (TNN was owned by CBS/Viacom.) CBS had Ken Squier and Mike Joy under contract, and they did the biggest races, but I got the chance to do a number of events, usually for the Busch Series or the Craftsman Truck Series.

My first gig was a midsummer double-header in Milwaukee. These are two-day events where the Busch Series runs one day and the trucks run on the other. I always enjoy working the Busch (now the Nationwide) Series, but I especially like working the truck races. The competition is superb.

Truck races are relatively short, usually running about an hour and forty minutes, so there is very much a sprint race mentality. The drivers go all out. There's a lot of strategy involved. The trucks really dirty up the air around them as they go around the racetrack, and they're boxy, much like stock cars from the '70s, so it's not unusual to see some of the maneuvers reminiscent of those days, like the old slingshot. Those moves are still very much alive in the truck series.

Back in Milwaukee I worked the booth with Ned Jarrett, and I don't mind admitting that before the race, I made it a point to have someone snap my picture holding a CBS microphone. I didn't know if I'd ever get a chance to work for CBS again (thankfully, I did), and I was thrilled. It had been my dream as a kid to someday work for one of the big networks, and now I was standing on the roof of the Milwaukee Mile, wearing my blazer with the CBS "eye" logo embroidered over the breast pocket, holding a CBS microphone, with senior CBS Sports producer Eric Mann talking to me in my ear. I hope I didn't say it out loud, but I was definitely thinking, *This doesn't suck.*

I had a few CBS race telecasts under my belt, when one day I got

It had been a lifelong dream to work for CBS. I was so proud!

a call at my home in Birmingham on a Friday afternoon. It was Terry Ewert, executive producer for CBS Sports. "What are you doing tomorrow?" he asked.

I was committed to do a University of Alabama basketball game and told him so. Then he asked if I could get out of it. Evidently, Jim Nantz, who was scheduled to do the play-by-play for a University of Arizona basketball game, had come down with laryngitis. So CBS was planning to send Tim Brando—who was scheduled to do the South Carolina–Georgia game the next day—to Tucson to do the Arizona game with Billy Packer, Nantz's partner on the broadcast. That left a hole in the South Carolina–Georgia game. And CBS wanted me to fill it.

My bosses at the University of Alabama graciously gave the OK for me to miss the Bama game and do the game for CBS. I immediately threw some stuff in my suitcase and headed for Athens, Georgia. Since both South Carolina and Georgia are in the Southeastern Conference, the same conference as Alabama, I was pretty familiar with the players from these schools, but I still needed to get up to snuff. When I arrived at my hotel, there was a big packet of information waiting for me, and I stayed up late, reading and memorizing information. To this day, I never go to bed unless I'm ready for the next day's broadcast. Some guys will wait till the next morning to finish preparing. But I can't do that. Not that I would have been sleeping much that night anyway!

The next morning, I went to the University of Georgia's Stegeman Coliseum to watch the teams during their game-day shootaround. I also met my broadcast partner for the game, which was none other than the legendary Al McGuire, the national championship winning coach from Marquette University who went on to become a superb broadcaster for both NBC and CBS. We had a quick lunch, then later met back at the coliseum for the pregame show.

Anyone involved in sports—players, coaches, broadcasters—often get asked if they have any pregame superstitions. Accomplished players, coaches, and broadcasters seem to get asked this question especially often, as if their answer might hold some magic secret to success.

When asked this question during his coaching days, McGuire used to answer that prior to the opening tip-off, he would always count the crowd.

The unsuspecting reporter would say, "Oh? For good luck?"

McGuire's response: "No. Because I get 5 percent of the house." He was a dandy.

Another oft-told story from McGuire's coaching days was that he focused so intensely on his own players that he didn't know the names of any players on rival teams. Not even the big stars. So I took no offense when, before the game, I saw McGuire jot down my name on a piece of paper. He wrote it in big, bright-red letters—*E-L-I*—and circled it. No doubt he wanted to have my name in his notes, just in case. I didn't take this personally. He was a Hall of Famer who worked with some of the biggest names in the business, including Tim Brando and Dick Enberg. He didn't know me from Adam's house cat. I didn't blame him for wanting to be prepared.

The broadcast got underway. At one point, we tossed it back to the studio in New York, and Michelle Tafoya did a cut-in from another game. When it came back to us, I said, "Thanks Michelle . . ." Then I led to McGuire, who planned to go directly into a segment where he would illustrate a play using the telestrator, the tool that allows you to "draw" on the screen. He was about to begin when he looked over to me, trying to include me in the discussion, and said, "You know . . ."

There was a long pause. I saw him searching through his notes. Obviously he was looking for my name but couldn't locate it, so he continued: "You know, *pal* . . ."

And "pal" I remained for the remainder of the broadcast. Which was fine with me. I was on CBS, working with Al McGuire. He could have called me anything he wanted.

Nothing is set in stone in the television sports business. Since the telecasts involve live events, sometimes it seems that nothing goes as planned. One football Saturday in the fall of 2001, Alabama played Ole Miss in Oxford, Mississippi, for an 11:30 a.m. kickoff. We'd just finished the postgame show. It was around four o'clock, and I was driving out of Oxford on my way home to Birmingham when my cell phone rang. It was a producer from Turner Broadcasting System (TBS).

"Hi, Eli. Where are you?"

I told him I was heading from Oxford to Birmingham.

He said, "Stop and make a U-turn."

I said, "What?"

He asked, "What are you doing tomorrow?"

I told him I had nothing scheduled.

He said, "We need you to work for Turner. Make a U-turn and head toward Memphis. I'll talk to you as you drive."

As it turned out, TBS was in Memphis to broadcast the NASCAR Busch Series race from Memphis Motorsports Park that day, but it was rained out. They were going to run the race the next day but the broadcast crew was due in Martinsville for the NASCAR Winston Cup race.

Neither NBC, which was broadcasting the Martinsville race, nor TBS, which was broadcasting the Memphis race, wanted to air the races simultaneously. This would only result in both networks losing viewers. So TBS decided to tape the Memphis race on Sunday and air it on Monday.

That's where I came in. I would do the play-by-play for the TBS broadcast in Memphis.

On Sunday morning I got to the track and changed into the TBS shirt I had been given. We were ready to go when just forty-five minutes prior to airtime, a guy came charging up to the booth and said, "It's raining in Martinsville, and the Winston Cup race is delayed. NBC made a deal to pick up our race here in Memphis!"

We all changed into plain, non-logoed shirts and sports jackets so no one was sporting a TBS logo. The stage manager scurried around, removing the TBS flags from the microphones and replacing them with the NBC mics. The Peacock it was!

Bill Weber and Allen Bestwick signed on from Martinsville, showing the obligatory rain shots—the umbrellas, the cars covered up. "There's rain in Martinsville, but don't worry, folks. NASCAR is still in business today. Yesterday's Busch race was rained out in Memphis, but they're about to begin right now. Here's Eli Gold in Memphis . . ."

And once again, I said words I never dreamed I would be saying: "You are watching NASCAR on NBC . . ."

As of the 2001 season, there was no longer NASCAR coverage on TNN. But since I was still under contract with the network, as were others on the broadcast crew, I shifted into doing other motorsports telecasts, which included drag racing and World of Outlaws events.

We did a year of World of Outlaws coverage on TNN, traveling to some of the smallest, most obscure racetracks that you've never heard of. They were fantastic events, and the venues were always packed with fervent fans. But many of the tracks were far, far off the beaten path.

One day I flew into Lincoln, Nebraska, where I met my assistant, Martha Oliver, so we could drive to the town of Eagle for the next day's race. Since we were in Nebraska, Martha suggested we go somewhere and find a really good steak. After all, this was the heart of beef country. I'm never one to pass up a good Porterhouse, so I thought that sounded fantastic. But I'm also a stickler for my routine. I like to get where I'm going, get checked into the hotel, and put my stuff away before venturing out. I insisted on driving to Eagle first.

I never would have imagined that there were no restaurants in the town. Not one. There was nothing but grain silos and the racetrack. So we got back in the car and drove to the interstate exit where we'd seen some lights. That night I took Martha to eat at the truck stop in Eagle, Nebraska. We both ordered cheeseburgers, and they weren't bad. At least we were eating beef in Nebraska. I'm still trying to live that one down.

The races really were exciting. How can they not be? The cars are so fast and light that they need big wings on their roofs just to keep them on the ground. One of the most spectacular races was at the Bristol Motor Speedway, where the owner, Bruton Smith, had his staff convert the famed asphalt track into a dirt track by covering it with plastic, then trucking in thousands of cubic yards of dirt. Those overpowered, winged sprint cars got around that half-mile-long track—with thirty-six degrees of banking—in thirteen seconds!

I realized there might be some resentment at the idea of a NASCAR broadcaster coming in and doing World of Outlaw events. But I sincerely did my best to give the fans the solid coverage they were due.

I tried to respect the sport as its own entity, resisting the urge to constantly compare it to NASCAR.

That said, there are quite a few NASCAR drivers with ties to the World of Outlaws. Kasey Kahne is involved. And of course, Tony Stewart is a graduate of the series and owns a team as well as the famous dirt track, the Eldora Speedway.

No question about it, Stewart is deeply passionate about the World of Outlaws. Within one hour of the announcement that I would be the new World of Outlaws announcer, my phone rang. It was Tony Stewart. He'd never called me before. Why would he call me?

He said, "Congratulations on your deal, pal."

(Here's another guy calling me "pal.")

Then he said, "I'm guessing you follow the sport but don't really know a whole heck of a lot about it."

Absolutely true.

He said, "Anything you need, I want you to pick up the phone and call me. I don't care how silly you think the question is; you will not be bothering me. I don't care if you have to call me twenty-five times."

He went on to say he would arrange for me to meet with Danny "the Dude" Lasoski, who drove for his team, so I could learn all about the cars. He genuinely cared that the sport he loved got the best treatment possible. Say what you want about Tony Stewart. Sure, he's been known to blow his top. But the guy speaks his mind. It's refreshing to encounter someone that sincere.

In addition to the World of Outlaws, I also did the play-by-play for NHRA (National Hot Rod Association) drag racing events for several years. I used to watch drag racing all the time, and over the years I had met drivers such as Don Prudhomme and Kenny Bernstein. The other broadcasters—Dave McClelland, Bob Frey, Bill Stephens, and Alan Reinhart among them—were wonderful people. They had forgotten more about the NHRA than I would ever know.

When you think of drag racing, you think of short bursts on a straight track. But there was nothing short about our broadcasts. On Sundays the races would begin at 11:00 a.m. with eliminations and often wouldn't wrap up until 6:00 or 7:00 p.m. We weren't on the air the entire time; we'd tape in segments, on and off, on and off, over a seven- or eight-hour time span. It was challenging to keep up the momentum.

One guy who never had trouble keeping up the pace was the aptly named John Force. With 126 victories and 14 Funny Car championships to his credit, Force is the undisputed king of the drag-racing world. He also lives up to his nickname, "Brute Force," on and off the track.

During my time with TNN, I did a show called *This Week in NASCAR*, which started out on the Prime Network (later Prime Ticket, then Fox Sports Net). The show was very much like a TV version of my radio call-in show *NASCAR Live!* except we had the guests live in the studio or on location.

NASCAR Vice-President Jim Foster (L) and driver Bill Elliott (C) join me on the set of "This Week In NASCAR"

Richard Childress (L) and Dale Earnhardt (C) share a laugh with me on "This week In NASCAR."

Dale Earnhardt was always a willing guest on both my radio and TV talk shows.

One weekend I was doing the drag race at Heartland Park in Topeka, Kansas, so I decided it would be fun to put together a mixed bag of guests and do *This Week in NASCAR* from that track. The premise of the show was to compare NASCAR and drag racing. My guests were drag-racing champion Don "the Snake" Prudhomme, former NASCAR team owner and drag-racing champion Kenny Bernstein, and John Force. Well, I had all sorts of plans to seed the conversation with questions about sponsorship, technology, and so on, but it just wasn't necessary.

Force took off like a rocket. He was hilarious. It was akin to having Robin Williams on the show. At one point, I looked at the camera and said, "Folks, I have no idea when I lost control of the program."

After that show, I never doubted that the man could indeed accelerate from 0 to 330 miles per hour in 4.6 seconds.

Laughing with NASCAR great Benny Parsons in Michigan

Football coach and part-time NASCAR racer Jerry Glanville was always ready to talk "shocks" and Xs and Os.

In costume shooting a series of TV spots for the Food Lion Supermarket Chain
(L-R): Bobby Labonte, Ken Schrader, Ken's daughter Dorothy, Eli the Pirate, my
daughter Elise, Terry Labonte, and a Food Lion rep.

A true thrill and an honor—interviewing legendary basketball coach John
Wooden at his tournament in Anaheim, California

Courtside for a Bama broadcast (L-R): Color man Tom Roberts,
yours truly, former Bama hoops great Reggie "Mule King," and
engineer/producer Tom Stipe

NFL Hall-Of-Famer Mike Ditka visits with us on the air at the Daytona 500

"I'm ready for my close up now, Mr. DeMille." In costume, complete with parrot on my left shoulder while shooting commercials for the Food Lion Supermarket chain.

ESPN's Dan Patrick hands me my Sportscaster of the Year award for the State of Alabama

THIRTEEN

In the Arena

WHEN I WAS WORKING AT TNN DOING NASCAR, AT ONE POINT network president David Hall decided to broaden the network's sports scope. So he secured the rights to broadcast games for the Arena Football League (AFL). When I heard this, I called him right away. Though David was the boss, he was the kind of guy you could pick up the phone and talk to. I told him I was ready to step in and start doing arena football immediately. I was experienced with the stadium-played game—I had been doing the University of Alabama football games for years—and I really wanted to do this. The AFL is similar to the NFL, but it's played indoors on a smaller field with somewhat different rules. It's quick; you have to strap an oxygen tank to your back to keep up. The field is only fifty yards in length, so the quarterbacks can throw from one end of the field to the other. There is a lot of scoring; it's not unusual to see scores of 70-60! They call arena football "the fifty-yard indoor war," and that's pretty accurate.

I was hired to do the AFL broadcasts on TNN along with color analysts Sam Wyche, the former Super Bowl coach of the Cincinnati

Bengals, and Ed Cunningham, a former Arizona Cardinals and Seattle Seahawks center, who was also working for CBS at the time.

Now I had to learn the game.

AFL games had not been broadcast on TV before, so I got tapes of the games that teams used for scouting purposes and studied them. We had meetings with the league officials to go over the rules. The reps from the AFL wanted us to be prepared and were incredibly helpful.

Working on AFL broadcasts for TNN, which I ended up doing for three years, turned out to be one of the best experiences I've ever had. It was awesome! TNN treated every week like it was the Super Bowl. There were as many as thirteen cameras on the field for every game. To this day, CBS will use fewer than that for a regional NFL game. We had robotic cameras and the latest and greatest in technology and innovative graphics. The broadcast quality was magnificent.

TNN didn't spare a dime, and that included travel. During the play-offs, we'd fly from Orlando to San Jose in fully catered private jets. During one cross-country trip, I settled into a seat near one of our producers, Emily Berman, and color analyst Mark May, the former Washington Redskins offensive lineman (one of the famous "Hogs"), while my spotter, Butch Owens, took a seat on the couch toward the back of the jet. To hear Butch tell it, he was giving me the better seat, but I beg to differ. At one point, our lovely sideline reporter, Jill Arrington, took a seat next to him. By the time the plane was flying over the panhandle of Texas, she had put a pillow on his lap and was resting her head there to take a nap. Me? I was hemorrhaging money in a card game. The hog led me to slaughter.

On road trips we'd always stay in four- and five-star hotels. When we got to the game city, we'd have luncheons with the local cable operators, just like they do in the NFL. It was first class all the way.

One of the most unusual components of the game is the giant nets at either end of the field. If the ball is thrown or kicked and it hits the net, it's live. If the quarterback throws the ball and misses his receiver and the ball hits the net and then comes careening back onto the field of play, it can be caught by either team. If an offensive player catches the ball, it's a completed pass. If a player on the defensive team catches the ball, it's an interception.

I still remember the final play of a play-off game in Phoenix where the Arizona Rattlers' quarterback, Sherdrick Bonner, threw a Hail Mary pass off the top of the net to his teammate, Chris Horn, who caught the ball as time expired for the win. That was classic AFL stuff.

Besides the game action, perhaps the best thing about broadcasting AFL games was the accessibility of the athletes and coaches. The players, many who later moved on to play in the NFL, craved national TV attention, so they were incredibly cooperative. Plus, the league allowed us to mic the players. This was really innovative at the time. Just a few seconds after a play, we could hear from the players directly!

One player who wore a microphone was a young Iowa Barnstormers quarterback named Kurt Warner. Here was a guy who had been working in a grocery store, stocking shelves before he got his break in the AFL. Of course, he soon went on to the NFL, where among his many achievements, he was named MVP after leading the St. Louis Rams to victory in Super Bowl XXXIV. And we had him wired!

Another great player was Hunkie Cooper, who played for the Arizona Rattlers and was arguably the best player to ever compete in the league. He was a magnificent athlete. In the AFL, players play both offense and defense, and this guy could do it all. He was a running back, linebacker, wide receiver—basically, whatever the coach needed him to be.

Once, during Arizona's play-off game against New England, we put a microphone on Hunkie. We had done this before and it was great. Unlike some players you had to watch out for, Cooper was fairly mild-mannered; a clean-cut guy who didn't habitually curse on the field. (The same went for Kurt Warner.) But during this particular game, things got heated between Cooper and New England's Charlie Davidson.

Cooper would make a great catch; then on the next play, Davidson would knock the ball away. They were going at each other all night. Trash-talking. Back and forth. Nonstop.

During the fourth quarter, Cooper made a magnificent circus catch. It was just spectacular. The audio guy turned up Cooper's microphone, and we were all watching and listening as Cooper, who was holding the football after this awesome catch, looked down at Davidson, who was on the ground, and said, "Take that, you @#$%# @#% @##*%!"

Well, this goes out on live TV. Sure, it was just cable TV, but it was live, and Hunkie Cooper, the guy who knew better than to curse, just peeled off a phrase that stopped us all dead in our tracks. I didn't know what to say. I mean, he not only strung together a series of bad words, but he'd ended the phrase with a racial epithet.

Sitting next to me was color analyst Mark May, who along with both Cooper and Davidson, just happens to be an African-American. I couldn't move. I just sat there stunned, staring straight ahead. I didn't even look at May out of the corner of my eye. Then, May saved the day when he said, "Folks, the emotion in this game is real! It's no different than in the NFL. But we apologize for the language. It should not have made our airwaves."

Later, down in the locker room, Hunkie Cooper's mom called him on his cell phone and read him the riot act: "Do you eat with that mouth? I raised you better . . ."

Cooper was mortified. He apologized to his teammates and coach. Then he went out to the TV truck and apologized to everyone he could find. He apologized to the truck driver. He apologized to Butch Owens and our statistician, Brian Roberts. He apologized to the guys hanging the wires. Everyone! Then, the next week he apologized to the viewers on the air. Really, the fault was ours. We should have delayed the audio from the players' mics. And indeed, after that incident we did!

I participated in the TNN broadcasts for three years until, as they say, the coverage was picked up by another network. I wanted badly to continue doing arena football for the other network, NBC, but since they had an excellent stable of play-by-play announcers already on staff, it was a long shot.

Even though representatives at the league were kind enough to put in a good word for me, and my agent was working hard on my behalf, the decision belonged to the network. It's understandable, from a budgetary standpoint, that they would want to use broadcasters (and extremely accomplished ones at that!) who were already on staff and on salary.

Then, a sad event resulted in a shift of the status quo in the broadcast world. In August 2002, Chick Hearn, the great Voice of the L.A. Lakers, passed away. Paul Sunderland, who was an NBC staff play-by-play announcer, got the call and accepted the offer to become the new Voice of the Lakers. That opened up a slot on the NBC roster.

Sunderland had been an NBC staff announcer, and although it was not official, it was almost a given that he would have been one of three announcers, along with Tom Hammond and Dan Hicks, doing the AFL games when the new season began in 2003. But now, Sunderland would be unavailable. So I got the call from the executive producer of NBC Sports, Tommy Roy. I was ecstatic. I said, "Yes! Yes! Yes!" before he even had the chance to say, "We'd like you to work for NBC, doing arena football."

One of the most appealing aspects of the job was the opportunity to once again work with my former partner on TNN, Charles Davis. I worked with some talented analysts at TNN. Ed Cunningham was superb. What a magnificent sense of humor. Once, we'd just gone

I never ever would have believed that I would be working for NBC Sports. I dreamed it, but never expected it.

on the air for an Iowa Barnstormers game, and I looked over, and Ed was wearing one of those old-time, barnstormer pilot caps, like Snoopy wore to fight the Red Baron. He didn't make reference to it. Just had it on his head. Completely deadpan.

The color analyst I worked with the longest was Charles Davis. We built up a fantastic rapport. These days Charles works for Fox Sports, the Big 10 Network, and the NFL Network, among other things, and he is one of the absolute best in the business! He annually does the color on the BCS National Championship Game telecast.

The guy has the sharpest mind. Not only does he know sports, but we'll be talking on the air and all of the sudden he'll be quoting Uncle Fester from *The Addams Family* or the professor from an episode of *Gilligan's Island*. His brain is full of useless trivia, much like my own, and we would battle back and forth, attempting to one-up each other.

It was funny how well we got along, since we should have been mortal enemies. Charles was a former defensive back for the University of Tennessee, the University of Alabama's biggest rival next to Auburn. We used to laugh about that all the time. How did a former Vols player and the Voice of the Tide end up in the booth together?

Charles had already been hired as an analyst for NBC's arena football coverage when I got the call. I really hoped to be working with him again.

So, before the start of the season, in the dead of winter—I remember it being bitter, bitter cold—NBC brought everyone involved with the broadcasts to the Nassau Coliseum on Long Island for a crash course in arena football. It was the start of training camp for the AFL, so they arranged to bring in a couple of teams, New York and Tampa, and have them play a series of exhibition games for some schoolkids and some fans.

The objective for the network was to give everyone—producers, directors, audio people, camera guys, and on-air talent—the opportunity to learn the game.

Arena football is so fast and has so many nuances that it takes some getting used to. The game is challenging at first, even for the best broadcasters. Tom Hammond is a great basketball man. He's also done college football, the NFL, horse racing, and track and field at the Olympics. But he had never done the AFL. Ditto for Dan Hicks. He's done everything, golf included, but he'd never done arena football. So this was a great idea.

We were divided into crews, and each group did broadcasts of the game. Charles and I worked together during our shift, and if I do say so myself, we nailed it. We had the advantage of experience. We were the only guys who had done arena football before, so we knew the history of the game; we knew the players, the tidbits, and the backstories.

But NBC didn't team us together at first. Since we were the only guys with experience, they split us up so we could work with other broadcasters who were new to the beat. Charles began the season working with Dan Hicks, while I was teamed with former NFL running back great John Riggins. After a while we were paired together again and later would have many opportunities to work together on regional telecasts for Comcast Sports and Fox Sports Net.

I did arena football for NBC for two full seasons and part of a third. What a great feeling it is to be standing by, waiting to go on the air, holding an NBC mic, and hear an Emmy award–winning producer say in your ear, "OK, you've got the whole country with you!" What a rush!

Although I didn't like it, I completely understood why NBC went back to using staff announcers for the remainder of their arena football broadcasts. Ratings were not good, and in an effort to cut back expenses, they were smart to use the announcers they were already paying. NBC had a revenue-sharing agreement with the AFL, and if they didn't have to pay freelance guys like me, there was more revenue to share.

A few years later, in 2009, the league went on hiatus. It's a challenge for arena football teams to make a profit, partly because arena football is still a niche sport. TV viewership was not great in cities without franchises. But in many cities with AFL home teams, ratings were through the roof! As was attendance. You couldn't get a ticket to see the Orlando Predators or the Arizona Rattlers back in the day. The Grand Rapids Rampage had a small building, just a nine- to ten-thousand-seat arena, but it was always sold out. The Iowa Barnstormers, when they were up and running, absolutely packed 'em in.

The good news is the AFL has a solid plan in place to resume play in 2010. Arena football? I'd do it again in a heartbeat.

In this business, you never know when and where your next opportunity will emerge. While working in the arena football world, I met and became friendly with Larry Kahn, who was the Voice of the AFL's Los Angeles Avengers. Larry had a long broadcasting résumé; among other things he was the Voice of the USC Trojans in the mid-'90s, and for years he did pre- and postgame shows for the Anaheim Angels, as well as the play-by-play for the Angels during the 1999 season.

In 1998 Larry started his own company, the Sports USA Radio Network, an independent national syndicator of sporting events, which, during its first season, broadcast just a few select college games, mostly bowl games on radio. In 2001 the schedule expanded to include a major college football game every week, and in 2002 Sports USA also began broadcasting NFL games.

One evening back in 2002, Larry and I ran into each other at the AFL banquet in Orlando, where I was serving as master of ceremonies. We were discussing his company when the conversation drifted toward another syndicator, whose name I won't mention, that does a lot of big-time sports on radio.

Comparing notes, we found that we both had similar past experiences with this company, which is a major player in the business. The people at this company would never answer your calls, letters, or e-mails. They wouldn't acknowledge the receipt of your audition tape, even with a form rejection letter. We both agreed that the way they did business was lame at best and rude at worst.

So I was glad that Larry would be giving these guys some competition. And I was especially glad when he asked me if I'd be interested in doing some NFL games.

I said, "Larry, I would crawl to an NFL stadium to do a game."

Several months later, Larry called. "Are you ready to do the NFL?"

I was. Larry hired me. I went on the road for him every Sunday, and despite my earlier declaration, he graciously did not make me crawl.

Prior to air time for a 49ers game at Candlestick Park in San Francisco

Sports USA is a fantastic operation. It has all the advantages of a small company (when you make your travel arrangements, you call Larry's wife, Nanci), along with the respect afforded a larger outfit (the network recently was asked to bid on the Monday Night Football radio package).

Currently, I do the play-by-play for one of Sports USA's NFL games

At Qualcomm Stadium in San Diego prior to a Chargers/Packers Broadcast

on Sundays. When the University of Alabama has an off week, I will do the occasional college game. Schedule permitting, I also do bowl games, such as the Capital One Bowl, the Insight Bowl, the Las Vegas Bowl, whatever.

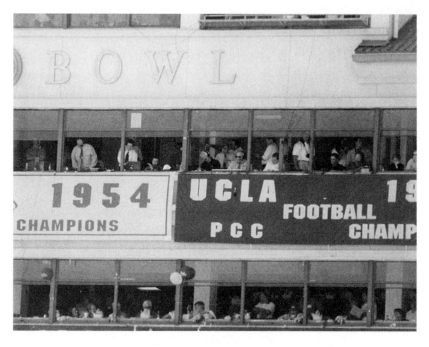

At the Rose Bowl for the Tide and the UCLA Bruins; our booth was right over the letters "UCLA."

After twenty-plus years doing the broadcasts for Alabama football games, people ask me if it's strange doing the play-by-play for another college game. My answer? It's not strange. But it's completely different.

When I'm doing the Alabama broadcasts, I want Alabama to win. I know all the players and live and die by what they do on the field each week. If Kansas is playing NC State or Boise State is playing Colorado, I don't care who wins. Or should I say, I'm not invested in the outcome. In that sense, it makes it a lot of fun.

It's rare that I would do another game in the SEC, which is Alabama's conference, but once I did a broadcast for the NCAA game of the week, which happened to feature Georgia at Tennessee.

My bosses at Alabama gave the OK for this, but I was still very sensitive and acutely aware of the fact that I was calling a game involving a school Alabama has played in the past (Georgia) and another that Alabama plays—and plays with great emotion—every year (Tennessee).

The Tennessee people were extremely accommodating. The sports information director, Bud Ford, said that I was welcome to do anything that any visiting broadcaster would expect to do, which included attending practice. Even so, I skipped practice, just so everybody would be comfortable, and on game day I did my darnedest to call that game right down the middle.

John Robinson, the longtime USC and L.A. Rams coach, was my color analyst for the Tennessee–Georgia game. Afterward, Robinson said, "If anybody tuned in to that broadcast and didn't already know you were the Alabama broadcaster, they would never have known. Helluva job."

I so appreciated that, because although I always try to call it straight, that day I wanted to call every play right down the middle.

In many ways NFL games are easier to do than college football games. NFL team rosters are much smaller than college rosters. Pro teams have fifty-four players, about half the number on a college team.

When Alabama plays Utah State, here comes Utah State, wandering into Tuscaloosa, with 105 guys you've never heard of!

If you follow the NFL, and I do, then you're already familiar with many of the players on all the teams. You don't have to look down at your notes to identify Peyton Manning or Alge Crumpler. If you're watching Arizona play, you don't even have to see his jersey to know that Edgerrin James just made that run. You recognize him from his stance, his body style, and his hair.

On the other hand, as compared to college games, NFL games move really fast. The pace is incredibly intense.

In the NFL there is less time between plays. The commercial breaks only last as long as the time-outs, usually a minute and thirty-five seconds or so. When you come out of a commercial break, the offensive team is already breaking the huddle to come to the line of scrimmage; whereas in college, the radio broadcast will take a minute or a minute-and-thirty-second break, and the TV network might be away for three minutes. So when we come back on the air during Alabama games, we have time to shoot the breeze, tell a story, do another commercial, sell something, whatever it is! The pace is far more relaxed. NFL games, on the other hand, run like clockwork.

One thing I definitely do on NFL Sundays is make it a point to stop and take it all in. I've been to just about every major stadium and arena in the country, but I still get a chill when I walk into these buildings.

I was actually looking forward to the chill the last time I worked at Lambeau Field in Green Bay, Wisconsin. I'd been to the legendary stadium before—several times for work and once a few years earlier, when my wife and I flew there just to watch a game. It was such an

The obligatory photo outside of Lambeau Field in Green Bay

Butch Owens and I in the booth in Lambeau prior to the Packers and the Denver Broncos game

Standing on the (un)frozen Tundra on the warmest Dec. 28th in Green Bay history

awesome scene—very much like an Alabama football game—with people spread out across acres of parking lots, cooking their bratwurst, drinking beer, and tailgating to beat the band. Of course, the major difference between an Alabama football game and a Packers game is the temperature.

When I found out that I, along with my spotter, Butch Owens, and statistician, Brian Roberts, would be traveling to Green Bay for a late-December game, we were all anticipating a frozen tundra–type experience. We wanted to see our breath in front of our faces, like the guys in all those NFL Films clips of the 1967 Ice Bowl. So we packed our warmest clothing and bought a dozen of those chemical packets you shake and put in your socks and gloves to keep warm. We were prepared! But when we got there on December 28, the day before the game, it was sixty-one degrees. Ditto the day of the game. It was the warmest December 28 and 29 in Wisconsin history.

Even though we did the game in our shirtsleeves instead of our thermal underwear layered under our fleece jackets and parkas, the game was a thriller. The Packers won their game against the Broncos, and since the Arizona Cardinals also won their game against the Detroit Lions the same day, the Packers were play-off bound.

As good as the game was, maybe the best part was flying into Green Bay and watching Butch's and Brian's reactions at seeing Lambeau Field from the air (this was their first time). They were genuinely excited, as I was the first time I saw the house that Lombardi built. We took the time to go through the Packers Hall of Fame, taking special care to look at memorabilia from two great Alabama-players-turned-Packer-stars, Don Hutson and Bart Starr. I wanted us all to take a moment and realize how lucky we were—and are.

I still do this. I always take a moment to appreciate the fantastic job I have. I think it's important to stop and take it all in (and yes, Aunt Stella, they do pay me for this!) whether I'm at Qualcomm Stadium in San Diego or the Daytona International Speedway or Madison Square Garden. Especially Madison Square Garden!

I've returned to the Garden dozens of times since my old peanut-selling, office-boy days of the late '60s and early '70s. But I still get a thrill from walking into the place. It doesn't matter if I'm a ticket-holding fan or if I'm there to broadcast that night's event; Madison Square Garden is just that special to me.

In 2006 I was hired as the radio play-by-play man for the Nashville Predators of the NHL. At one point, the team traveled to New York for a five-night stretch, playing the Islanders on Long Island, the Devils in New Jersey, and the Rangers in New York City.

On the day the Predators were scheduled to play the Rangers, I arrived at the Garden four hours before face-off just to sit in the seats and stare at the MSG logo, then stare at the jerseys hanging from the rafters: Rod Gilbert, Willis Reed, Walt "Clyde" Frazier, Eddie Giacomin . . .

As corny as it sounds, this is what keeps me motivated. If ever I get to feeling lazy or if I don't want to prepare or if I just can't stand to look at another depth chart or stats sheet, all I have to do is remember that great feeling of walking into an arena. I remind myself how special the feeling is when I walk into the great buildings in Boston, Toronto, Philadelphia, and Los Angeles. I remember Roger Doucet singing "O Canada" and "The Star-Spangled Banner" before a Canadiens game at the old Montreal Forum. I imagine the dropping of the puck and the sound of skates cutting across the ice. Then, reenergized, I get back to work.

When I was working for the Birmingham Bulls back in the late 1970s, I got to know a gentleman named David Poile, who was then the assistant general manager for the Atlanta Flames. He later moved on to be the general manager for the Washington Capitals. Many seasons later, in the fall of 1997, I was in Nashville for an Alabama football game against Vanderbilt when I ran into David, who had just been named general manager of the Nashville Predators, one of the new NHL expansion teams. At the time, he was busy assembling the roster and generally getting his team ready for their debut.

He said, "Any interest in coming back and doing hockey?"

I said, "Man, I'd love to."

But the Preds were looking for someone—appropriately so—who lived in Nashville and would be available full-time to speak to chamber of commerce meetings and make other public appearances.

Regretfully, that was a deal breaker for me. So we both moved on, and I didn't give it another thought.

Almost ten years later, I crossed paths with Erik Barnhart, a guy I worked with back at TNN, who was now the director of broadcasting for the Predators. He asked me the same question David asked years earlier. Only this time, a move to Nashville was not part of the equation. And this time my answer was yes.

The Predators had been doing a simulcast, meaning they did one broadcast for both radio and television. This is a cost-saving measure for the team because they only have to pay one crew. But a simulcast is never ideal. The viewers and listeners get cheated. If you're doing a radio call also being shown on TV, then you're talking too much. If you're doing play-by-play geared for TV but it's also going out over radio, then the radio audience has no idea where the puck is. Nobody wins.

So in 2006, the Predators decided to split the broadcast. Now they would need a crew for both radio and TV, and they brought me in to do the radio.

The first thing I did was contact Pete Weber, the current Voice of the Predators. I'd known Pete forever, going back to when I was with the St. Louis Blues and he was with the Los Angeles Kings. I didn't want him to hear anything through the grapevine or have him think I approached the team and was trying to spin him out. Pete was wonderful. He'd already heard the team was splitting the broadcast, and he and color man Terry Crisp welcomed me aboard.

Terry Crisp played ten seasons in the NHL for the Boston Bruins, St. Louis Blues, New York Islanders, and Philadelphia Flyers, and coached eleven seasons in the NHL for the Philadelphia Flyers, Calgary Flames, and Tampa Bay Lightning. His name is on the Stanley Cup three times. And he's a Canadian. So his hockey résumé is beyond reproach. And personally, I love the guy.

"Crispy" and his wife, Sheila, are wonderful people and were as helpful as could be when I started with the Preds. The same goes for Pete Weber and his wife, Claudia. My wife and I became such good friends with them, and this almost—not quite, but almost—erased all my bad memories of color-man-turned-tormentor Gus Kyle back in my St. Louis Blues days.

Although I only worked for the Preds for one full year and a few games the following season, after which they went back to doing a simulcast, during those few months I may have laughed more than I ever have in my entire life. That's what happens when you throw a bunch of grown-ups together whose job it is to talk about other grown-ups playing a kids game.

Once, before I joined the team, the broadcast crew was on a bus heading from the hotel to the Phillips Arena, where the Predators were playing the Atlanta Thrashers. Everything was quiet when producer Bob Kohl, aka "Helmut," piped up. "Hey, where's the Georgia Dome from here?"

People thought he was joking because right in front of the bus was the seventy-one-thousand-seat behemoth of a Teflon-topped build-ing that is the Georgia Dome. It is one of the largest indoor sporting

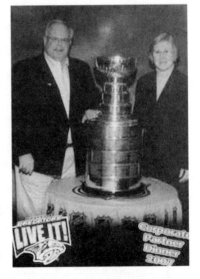

Claudette and I visit with the Stanley Cup during its stop in Nashville.

facilities in the country, and it was right there. But Bob wasn't joking. He just didn't see it.

From that day on, no matter what city we were in, the moment we caught sight of a large sports venue—for instance, the Anaheim Angels Stadium—someone would say, "Hey, where's the Big A from here?"

The season after I left the Preds, the guys still called me from the road. They'd be on the team bus going from the Detroit airport to the hotel, riding right past the old Tiger Stadium, and I'd answer, and it would be Pete Weber clearing his throat, then saying, "Hey, where's Tiger Stadium?"

If you said something—or did something—a little foolish around this bunch, you would never live it down. Once, the crew was staying in Manhattan Beach, California, following a game against the L.A. Kings and just prior to a game against Anaheim. I was sitting in my room, enjoying the afternoon off, when suddenly, someone banged on my door. I looked through the peephole, and all I saw was what appeared to be skin. Just naked flesh.

I couldn't make out anything, so I said, "Who is it?"

"Eli! Eli! It's me! Open the door! Hurry!"

I opened the door and it was our production engineer, who happened to be an extremely big man. I'm a big man. But he is B I I I I I I I G. He's one of the few people around who makes me look small. And there he stood. Wearing nothing but an extremely skimpy pair of underwear.

He ran past me and sat down. "Shut the door!"

Evidently he had ordered room service, finished his meal, and gone to put the tray outside, when the door shut behind him, leaving him outside with no room key—and wearing nothing but his skivvies.

When I was able to quit laughing, I called the front desk.

"Ma'am, this is Mr. Gold. There is a naked man sitting at the end of my bed who has locked himself out of his room. Would you mind bringing up a key to room 423? And please hurry."

The production engineer was mortified. "Please don't tell everybody!"

Well, I didn't tell *everybody*. I just told Pete Weber. And that was as good as making a video and posting it on YouTube or calling the Associated Press. We all had a good laugh over that story for months. Actually, years!

I got spoiled during my year with the Preds, because for the first time in my life, I was traveling regularly with a hockey team on their chartered aircraft. In the minors we took the bus. When I was with the Blues, I traveled separately to meet the team. But with the Preds, we boarded a chartered Midwest Express jet for our road trips. We all had our regular first-class seats on the plane. The players sat in the back, the coaches sat in the middle, and the broadcasters and support people sat up front. Being a creature of habit, I always took the same seat, my favorite, 1B. The graphics person, Linda P. Davis, would take the seat to my left.

Then, during one trip the flight attendant said to me, "That must be the broadcaster's favorite seat."

I said, "Why's that?"

She said, "That's where Bob Uecker always sits."

As it turned out, the jet the Predators leased was the same aircraft leased by the Milwaukee Brewers.

So, despite the fact that I'd never met the man, it turns out our rear ends had been sharing the same chair for months.

I miss working for the Preds. I miss the games against the Red Wings, where both teams were chasing each other in the standings for the Central Division. I miss the people. I miss the laughs. The only things I don't miss are naked guys banging on my door.

I love San Francisco. It is one of the big cities that I could live in.

Who booked this hotel, anyway? (Checking out the accommodations at Alcatraz)

My daughter Elise couldn't make this trip to San Francisco, but I made sure she heard the Sea Lions at Pier 39.

When in San Diego one MUST visit the world renowned San Diego Zoo.

FOURTEEN

High on the Tide

A YEAR OR TWO AFTER I MOVED TO BIRMINGHAM BACK IN THE late '70s, my friend, Butch Owens, took me to my first Alabama football game. I admit it. At first I couldn't imagine what all the fuss was about. I grew up in New York City, where everyone followed pro teams. I don't think I ever heard a college football game on the radio in Brooklyn. Certainly not a local one. Columbia University was lucky to win one game all year, and although my father once took me to a Notre Dame game at Yankee Stadium, college football wasn't exactly the talk of the town. I remember Butch's mother telling me long before we arrived in Tuscaloosa to watch the Crimson Tide play the Miami Hurricanes that day, "We're not leaving until the game is over. No matter what!"

Believe me. I got it. And quick.

In the spring of 1988 I was on the road when word came out that the current Voice of the Crimson Tide, Paul Kennedy, was not going to be rehired after the expiration of his five-year contract. Kennedy had followed the legendary John Forney into the role, and Forney, who had been behind the microphone for twenty-nine years, was a tough act to follow.

The next day there were articles in the paper about the situation. One story included a long list of candidates for the job. The last name on the list? Eli Gold. The funny thing was, I had never spoken to anyone at the university about the job. So this was news to me.

Over the next few days there were stories in the paper that said the candidates had been whittled down and the short list included yada yada, yada yada, and Eli Gold. I still hadn't spoken to anybody. Then, a few days later, a story ran listing the names of those coming in for interviews. Once again, Eli Gold was included. I still hadn't talked to anyone at the university, but I wasn't about to miss this chance, so I called Tommy Limbaugh, the associate athletic director at Alabama, who was heading the search for the new Voice of the Tide.

I said, "Mr. Limbaugh, you don't know me. My name is Eli Gold, and according to the newspapers, I'm coming down for an interview."

We both had a chuckle, and he said, "Well, would you like to?"

The very next day I met with him, and then I met with basketball coach Wimp Sanderson and football coach Bill Curry. During the meetings I was told that John Forney, who had been replaced by Paul Kennedy five years ago, would be coming back to resume his position as the Voice of the Tide. But John would just be doing the football broadcasts. The university decided to split the broadcast position between John and me, with John doing football and me doing basketball.

Well, I was elated. In the state of Alabama, working for the university is *the* sportscasting job to have, and I was thrilled to be hired. The fans were ecstatic to have John Forney back. He was a wonderful man and truly beloved. His voice accompanied the greatest moments in Alabama football history—from Coach Paul W. "Bear" Bryant's 315th win, to the Run-in-the-Mud, to the Goal Line Stand—and fans identified with him. Also, I found him to be an absolute gentleman. He treated me well, and I thought at the time that this was the very definition of a win-win situation.

During my first season broadcasting Alabama basketball games, I spent most every Thursday and part of Fridays at NASCAR tracks, working for MRN. Then on Friday nights I would fly to wherever the Alabama basketball team was playing that weekend, whether it was Tuscaloosa or somewhere on the road, then do the game on Saturday. After the game I would fly back to the racing city and broadcast the NASCAR race on Sunday.

One week in February 1989, Tommy Limbaugh called me on a Thursday night. He found me at my hotel in Richmond, Virginia, which was the race city that week, and asked if we could meet the next day in Knoxville at Alabama's basketball practice. I said, "Sure."

Immediately, I was concerned. Why would my boss come all the way to Knoxville to tell me something face-to-face? It was either very bad news—this isn't working out, thank you, see ya, good-bye—or it was very good news. I considered the possibility that he was going to offer me the football job, but I convinced myself it was probably something else.

The next day I woke up in Richmond to a blanket of snow. The airport was closed, and I had two big problems: one, I needed to be in Knoxville for a basketball game the next day; and two, I had agreed to meet Tommy Limbaugh that afternoon at the University of Tennessee's arena. I had to be there!

Due to the bad weather, my commercial flight was canceled, but I found a guy who knew a pilot. We agreed on a fee, and I hopped into the guy's little private plane. I don't remember if it was a Bonanza, a Piper Cub, or what, but I do know that we were the very first plane off the ground that morning when the airport reopened. The runway wasn't even totally cleared yet! A few hours later I was sitting at midcourt, about sixteen rows up, in the Thompson-Boling Arena with Tommy Limbaugh. After we exchanged a few pleasantries, Tommy, with a very resolute look on his face, looked at me and asked if I would accept the job as the Voice of the Crimson Tide football team. I agreed instantly.

From the day of the announcement in February until the start of the season in September, the university and I took a lot of heat. Part of the reason for this was the fact that John Forney was so beloved in Alabama. Many fans didn't want to see him go, but he had been in ill health, and after he finished his thirtieth year behind the microphone, it was decided that the time was right to make a change. I had lived in Alabama for ten years and had broadcast University of Alabama basketball for a year, but still, most people knew me as a pro sports guy. I did NASCAR, pro baseball, pro hockey. I was not yet perceived as part of "the family."

People wrote to the administration and said that if I was hired, they would stop contributing money to the university. Some said they would take the university out of their wills. Some people came and said that they thought my hiring was an absolute disgrace.

I was a young broadcaster who got lucky enough to land one of the most coveted jobs in the entire country, and some of my colleagues in the media took this as an opportunity to tar and feather me. At one point I simply stopped listening to sports talk radio. As for the newspapers, there was one guy in particular who complained that I wasn't an Alabama fan because I didn't even bother to attend the 1988 Iron Bowl. What he failed to mention, though, was that I was not there because I was out of town, broadcasting basketball for the Crimson Tide on November 25, 1988. What should have been one of the most exciting times of my life turned out to be a very stressful time. And the highest point on the stress-o-meter was my first Alabama football broadcast in the fall of 1989.

When I was first hired, the fact was, I had scant football experience. I'd done only a handful of games, and I knew my every word and every nuance would be scrutinized, so for my first game, the pressure was really on. I've never been more terrified of anything in my entire life. Not my first day at NBC, CBS, or ESPN. Nothing even came close.

I always overprepare anyway, but you better believe that day I was beyond prepared. And of course I got to the stadium—that particular game was at Legion Field—hours early. So that gave me way too much time to contemplate things and only added to my nerves. By game time, I was an absolute basket case.

I was shaking and trembling so badly that I literally could not hold my pen to write notes. I don't remember ever being that out of control of my body, before or since.

Once the broadcast began, things got a bit better. I remember other broadcasters telling me that you're a far better broadcaster when your team wins, so I'm grateful that Alabama beat Memphis State that day!

I never wear head gear and rarely do I wear sunglasses while working except when at Ole Miss for an early kickoff. The sun is blinding until midday.

Of course, things only got better and better.

Looking back, I'm glad to say, that early rough period upon being hired as the Voice of Crimson Tide is now just a distant memory. The experience since then has been nothing short of amazing. For fifteen years I did the play-by-play for both Crimson Tide basketball and football. Obviously, there are many, many differences between the two sports. For a broadcaster, one of the most significant differences is where you sit.

During football games you sit way up high in a booth. I always work with the windows open, no matter how hot or cold it is, so I can feel the wind and the weather and hear the crowd and the action on the field. During basketball games the announcers usually sit courtside. A slightly elevated position is best because you can spot defenses a little better without having to look around the referee or through a bunch of people's legs or bodies flashing in front of your face.

During conference or NCAA tournaments, the broadcast crew's courtside position is based on their team's seeding (the ranking determined by NCAA officials prior to the tournament). The better your team, the better your position. There were many games over the years where Bama was not the best team but not the worst team—in other words, right in the middle. So we'd be seated at the free-throw line extended, and there would be an official standing right smack in front of my face. I'd have to look around Gerald Boudreaux's rear end just to see the play!

Often our position was right next to the bench, where, for all practical purposes, we were part of the game. I've caught many bouncing basketballs over the years, and more than a couple of players. From the press table, you can hear every word, every grunt, and every bit of trash talk. You can literally reach out and touch the fans, the players, and the coaches. But that works both ways. The fans, players, and coaches can also reach out and touch you.

Once, Alabama was playing a game at the Otis Spunkmeyer Classic in Oakland against Texas Christian University (TCU). Somehow, our crew ended up sitting right next to TCU's bench. To my left was engineer Tom Stipe, to my right was color analyst Tom Roberts, and to his right was TCU's coach, Billy Tubbs.

The game was underway when the coach, a very nice, friendly guy, struck up a conversation with me. That would have been fine except for the fact that we were on the air.

He could hear every word of our broadcast, and as he walked back and forth in his coaching box, which was directly in front of me, he'd say, "You're doing a good job, Eli!"

Since I was on the air, I'd answer him back, "Thanks, Coach. Folks, that was Coach Billy Tubbs stopping by to say I was doing a good job . . ."

It kept on.

He'd say, "Man, Eli, you guys got a break on that one! You're not going to tell your audience that was a good call, are you?"

I'd say, "Coach, I thought it was a good call."

He'd say, "C'mon!"

We kept up the banter throughout the game, and although it gets dicey when you're talking about the referee's calls, we didn't even come close to getting a technical.

When broadcasting college basketball games, I had to keep my guard up, even after the game clock ran down. During the NCAA tournament one year, Alabama played Stanford at what was then called Riverfront Coliseum (now U.S. Bank Arena) in Cincinnati. The Tide won the ball game, which earned them the right to play North Carolina in the next round.

At many of these national postseason tournaments, there are so many reporters and broadcasters at the games that they have to build risers along the side of the court. Everybody sits on chairs on the risers, which are stacked three or four rows high.

After the game, I was about to interview Bama's assistant coach, David Hobbs (who later became head coach), for the postgame show. Hobbs pulled up a plastic chair next to mine, and because he didn't like to wear a headset, I grabbed a stick mic so I could hold it for him.

We began the interview, and as we talked, I started to relax. Bama won the game. Everybody felt good. I had been sitting in the same position for hours, so I started to stretch and lean back in my chair.

Well, unbeknownst to me, the riser, which was on wheels, had moved a few inches away from the hockey dasher boards, which had been kept in place during the tournament. There was a space. So when I pushed my chair back, the legs of the chair fell off the riser and got wedged between the riser and the dasher boards. Of course, I'm a big guy, and as soon as those rear legs went off the riser, the rest of the chair followed. The chair went down, little shards of plastic flew everywhere, and I tumbled over.

The incredible thing was, when I landed, I was still holding the mic! So, Hobbs, whose answer had been interrupted, calmly reached over, grabbed the wire, raised the microphone back up, took it in his hand, and continued talking as though nothing had happened! We were on radio, so no one was the wiser.

This incident marked the only time I broke the broadcaster's cardinal rule: never let the subject grab the mic. I read this tip in Marv Albert's book years before and took it to heart! But this time I made an exception and was grateful for Hobbs's grace under pressure.

While he continued talking, I climbed to my knees. When he finished his story, I retrieved the microphone while still kneeling on the riser and said, "We'll be right back . . ."

When it comes to basketball, you don't usually expect delays.

Games are indoors, so weather is not a factor. Usually, things run like a top. But there must have been a full moon the night top-ten-ranked Alabama traveled to Kansas to play the unranked Wichita State Shockers. Everything that could go wrong did go wrong.

During the first half, Alabama fell behind. They played poorly. Indeed, they looked like the unranked team! They didn't even win the opening tip-off. At the half, Bama was down by twenty-one points, and the Wichita State coach was so ecstatic that when the buzzer sounded, he threw his arms in the air, jumped off the bench, and landed awkwardly, ripping his ACL. He was hurt and fell to the floor, where he started flapping around like a fish out of water.

It took some time, but the EMTs tended to the coach, then finally helped him off the court. So halftime was delayed a bit. The thing was, halftime was already scheduled to go long because Wichita State had a special presentation. This was the night they were unveiling their new mascot. Actually, the mascot, Wushock, which is a humanized version of a shock of wheat, was the same. But the costume was new. Better, more colorful, more modern.

During the presentation they brought out every living person who had ever worn the Wushock costume over the years. There must have been thirty-five former Wushocks at mid-court, and they ranged from age 22 to, seemingly, 122. They introduced them all. ". . . And now, joining us from Topeka, where he's an attorney for the law firm of Barr, Barr and Bradshaw, here's Bill Bradshaw!"

Finally, the second half got underway. Bama inbounded the ball to Marcus Webb, a big, burly player who later played for the Celtics for one year (1992–93). Webb dribbled down the court and jammed the ball into the rim, ripped down the basket, and totally obliterated the backboard.

The building, Levitt Arena, did not have the modern type of back-board assembly where you could just roll in a new one and set it up.

This was the old kind of backboard that was attached to a cantilevered series of metal rods. It curved out over the court, and the basket and backboard hung down in the correct position. Further, they didn't have a replacement at the arena. But they did have one at the university rec center, somewhere across campus. So while a crew cleaned up the glass (and the guest Wushocks visited the concession stands), the Shockers dispensed some guys to get the replacement.

This would take a while, and that night I was working without a color man. With so much time to fill, I started interviewing everybody and his brother. I'd bring over newspaper guys, including Neal Sims, who was with the *Birmingham News*. I talked to absolutely everyone I could find.

They finally brought in the replacement basket, but the new unit didn't have a place to mount the shot clock. So they had to find a place to mount the shot clock. This, too, took a while. Finally, the second half continued. To make the evening longer than it already was (it was pushing midnight), Alabama lost badly.

The newspaper reporters were past their deadlines, so they gathered around while I interviewed Alabama head coach Wimp Sanderson for the postgame show. This way they could get their quotes directly from the coach's answers during the broadcast.

Sanderson coached at Alabama from 1981 to 1992. He won SEC Coach of the Year in '87, '88, and '90 and was named National Coach of the Year in 1987. He's a wonderful guy, but when you get to know him, you learn that even when he's happy, he scowls. But this night, the scowl was for real.

I said, "Coach, obviously being one of the most bizarre nights you've ever spent in a basketball arena, can you summarize what the heck happened tonight?"

He started talking, but he never raised his head. Mumbling to the floor, he said, "I can't believe what I saw here tonight . . ."

None of us could. And I for one never imagined a scenario where a game would be delayed on account of wheat.

As I've said, in basketball, broadcasters get to be in the thick of things. We are inches away from not only the court but also the crowd. In college basketball, this includes the pep band. And Ole Miss had a great one.

The band was spirited and played great. They were nice kids. The only problem was, at the Tad Smith Coliseum (aka the Tad Pad) in Oxford, Mississippi, they sat right behind our broadcast crew. I'm all for great atmosphere, but it's hard to be heard when you've got tubas, trumpets, and trombones literally just a few feet away.

So at one of the SEC broadcasters' meetings, I brought it up with Langston Rogers, the sports information director for Ole Miss. I told him that some of us had talked about it and wanted to ask him if there would be any way to relocate either our position or the location of the band.

Langston was absolutely great about it, and the next time Alabama played at the Tad Pad, lo and behold, we found that they had built a small riser across the arena floor. Now the visiting broadcasters were positioned across the floor, away from the band.

We showed up for the game and Langston said, "Hope you like your new spot!" We did, indeed.

I went about my business preparing for the broadcast. I was immersed in my work, looking at notes, memorizing numbers, and doing other pregame stuff. Then, an hour before tip-off, it was time for the pregame show. Our engineer, Tom Stipe, was counting us down per normal: "Two minutes . . . one minute . . . thirty seconds . . ." The music rolled. Tom took his index finger and pointed to me, which meant, "You're on!"

The second Tom pointed at me and I started to say, "Good evening, everybody," I heard the most unbelievable noise—the loudest, proudest version of the Ole Miss fight song ever to be played.

I spun around, and much to my amazement, the entire pep band had formed a semicircle around me.

While I was engrossed in my work, I hadn't noticed them walking over to my side of the court. They'd crept over one by one so I wouldn't notice them and got in position just in time to help welcome me to the airwaves.

I looked over and Langston Rogers, one of the nicest guys in the business, was laughing his fool head off.

Of course the band immediately went back to their position directly across from me. I couldn't help grinning and waving at them throughout the game. They got me good.

Regardless of the sport, for me, every broadcast has one thing in common: the set-up. I am beyond meticulous about how I lay out my papers and pens, position my microphone, and, in every sport but basketball, where I put my binoculars. This isn't about superstition. It doesn't go that deep. It's simply about knowing where everything is at all times. I'm a freak about it. NASCAR-crew-chief-turned-broadcaster Larry McReynolds used to tell me, "Man, I ought to sell tickets to let folks watch you set up like this." He's calling *me* pedantic? A guy whose job involved following engine specs to $1/100^{th}$ of an inch?

No matter what booth I'm in, everything has to be in its exact spot. I tape down the wires, lay out the papers, position my colored pens, and if something isn't exactly straight, I'll move it. Nobody understands this better than my spotter, Butch Owens.

I met Butch when I first moved to Birmingham and was doing hockey for the Birmingham Bulls. He was involved with the Bulls' booster club, and we bonded as fellow hockey fans and friends. When I was hired to do the Alabama football broadcasts, I brought Butch in as my spotter halfway into my first season. He's been with me ever since, not just for Alabama games but for arena football and NFL games as well. He's never missed a broadcast in twenty-plus years.

Using the chart I prepare ahead of time, Butch will point to the name of the player who just made a tackle or the number of the player who just made a great block so I can add it to my commentary. He'll pass me notes; he'll jot down statistics and tidbits and hand them to me.

Since we can't talk to each other during the broadcast, we work with a system of hand signals. When Butch makes a fist with his right hand and hits it into the open palm of his left hand, he's pointing out an exceptionally hard hit. If he makes a fist and thrusts his arm out, he's telling me there was a good block.

However we communicate, basically Butch functions as the other half of my brain. He knows what I want before I know what I want. We finish each other's sentences. It's a little scary, actually.

(L-R) Butch Owens, The Snake, and Ol' "What's His Name"

Me and my guys. My long-time spotter Butch Owens (standing) and statistician Brian Roberts (R) have traveled the country with me as the best support crew a broadcaster could ever ask for.

One of my nicknames for Butch (besides Butchie) is Charlie Hodge, who was Elvis Presley's right-hand man. That's what I call him, although I freely admit that my requests are much less exciting than those of the King. It doesn't matter whether I need my favorite soft drink smuggled into a stadium that is sponsored by my favorite soft drink's competitor, or whether I need a tissue because I have to blow my nose but can't leave my chair, Butch always comes through.

Once we arrived in Nashville for a football game against Vanderbilt. As always, we were in the press box three hours before kickoff, but for the first time I can ever remember, I opened my briefcase and didn't have my pushpins. And I have to have pushpins. Along with my chart, the pins help me keep track of who is in the ball game at any given time.

Being the great friend he is, Butchie went out on foot, in the freezing cold, to the university bookstore to buy some pushpins.

But the store was closed. So he walked a few blocks and found a

Kinko's. They were open but didn't sell pushpins. He walked a few more blocks and came to a drugstore. Incredibly, they didn't sell pushpins. They had thumbtacks, but no pushpins.

While he was walking back toward the stadium, he spotted a funeral home. Not wanting to fail in his mission, he walked in and found a woman working in the back office. He said, "Ma'am. I'm fixin' to ask you the dumbest question you've ever been asked. But do you have any pushpins? If so, I'll be happy to pay you for them. As many as you've got."

Well, the woman at the funeral home did have pushpins. A brand-new, unopened box of them. Butchie paid for them and hoofed it back to the stadium. And to this day, those are the pushpins I have in my briefcase.

The Crimson Tide Sports Network booth is in the foreground during a night game in Tuscaloosa's Bryant-Denny Stadium.

Like Butch, statistician Brian Roberts also works with me on all my football broadcasts—Alabama, NFL, all of them. As I've said before, the guy is a walking, talking Univac computer. He's been with me since 2002, when he replaced his father, Tom Roberts, who switched from statistician to sideline reporter. Brian didn't get this job because of his last name; he got it because he is really, really good.

Brian is not only accurate and quick, but he has an uncanny feel for what statistical tidbit would fit into a broadcast at any given moment. He knows how to dig up details that you just can't find by thumbing through pages in a media guide. There's always extra stuff, extra tidbits, and trends he comes up with. It's uncanny how he does it, but Brian does. I've come to trust and completely depend on Brian.

Tom Roberts has been with the Crimson Tide Sports Network for thirty years. Before that he was a news director at TV stations in Birmingham, so I guess it's safe to say that the guy is a lifelong broadcaster. His role at the network has changed many times over the years; he's like the utility man. He can do most anything!

Tom has done color analysis for both basketball and football. He has produced and hosted coaches' shows on both TV and radio. For several years he was the sideline reporter for our football broadcasts, and currently, he is on the air as the host of our pregame show, halftime show, and postgame show, among his many other duties for the network. The guy truly can do it all, but the one thing that has really impressed me over the years is Tom's ability to not crack up during an interview.

A few years back, Alabama was playing over in Hawaii, and Jim Nabors, the man who portrayed Gomer Pyle on the old *Andy Griffith Show* and his own show, *Gomer Pyle USMC*, came over to Aloha Stadium to watch the game. Nabors, a native of Sylacauga, Alabama, and proud graduate of the University of Alabama, has been living in Hawaii for years, where he owns an enormous macadamia nut farm.

Evidently, awhile back he had purchased umpteen number of acres of Pacific frontage land and become the primary supplier of macadamia nuts to the Mauna Loa Macadamia Nut Company. (And you only thought he was funny and he could sing.)

At one point during our show, Tom interviewed Nabors. After telling the folks at home about his six hundred acres of land and making sure to pepper in plenty of "Shazams!" Nabors detailed the nuts and bolts, if you will, of his thriving business.

Pearl Harbor serves as the backdrop for this shot of the Crimson Tide Sports Network Crew at Aloha Stadium in Honolulu. (L-R) Engineer/Producer Tom Stipe, Spotter Butch Owens, Broadcast host Tom Roberts, my sidekick Kenny Stabler, and yours truly.

Tom and Linda Roberts enjoying the Hawaiian Islands

"My daddy always said, take care of your nuts and your nuts will take care of you," he said. "You've got to take care of your nuts! I'm always good to my nuts . . ."

Tom couldn't speak. But to his credit, he never laughed.

During that same visit to Hawaii, Nabors brought Hawaiian entertainer Don Ho up to the booth.

Evidently, Ho was a huge Oakland Raiders fan and wanted to meet my color man, Kenny "the Snake" Stabler, who led the Oakland Raiders to victory during Super Bowl XI back in 1977.

Well, the minute we saw Ho, the Snake and I burst into a rendition of "Tiny Bubbles." I'm sure Ho has endured this from many people in the past, but he was a great sport about it. In fact, he couldn't have been any nicer.

Tom and I are on the air for the pre-game show from Aloha Stadium in Honolulu.

A few years later, in April 2007, I was in San Jose, California, working a Nashville Predators–San Jose Sharks hockey game, when I heard that Don Ho had passed away. Since he had lived in Oakland for part of his life and still had family there, I thought it was worthy of a mention. While on the air, I shared that I had a chance to meet Ho in Hawaii a few years back. Then I said, "I'd like to offer my condolences to Mrs. Ho and all the . . ."

Then I stopped. I realized I was about to add a clip to the blooper reel, so I rewound and said, ". . . members of Don Ho's family."

But I digress.

Engineer and producer Tom Stipe has been setting up the equipment and turning the dials for Alabama football games for twenty-six years. He worked with John Forney and Paul Kennedy. And now, for twenty years, he's worked with me!

In addition to his duties on football Saturdays, he's been the longtime engineer for basketball games and for the coach's call-in shows. He's the guy who shows up the day before the game and sets up all the equipment, keeps it running during the game, and breaks it all down after the game. Then the next week, he does it all again. It's a really tough and essential job, and I for one am glad it's Tom doing it!

Another of his duties, although it's not official, is to get in my ear and give me a line to say. I call him my private spinmeister. I'll be saying something on the air, and Tom will pop in my ear with a thought or a line, and more often than not, it's something I use.

I believe I have the absolute best support team that money can buy. I'm a much better broadcaster because of all these great people. Though I don't tell them, lest their heads get too big, I count my blessings every day they're around.

I'd be remiss if I didn't mention another gentleman who sat with us in our broadcast booth for years, our distinguished producer emeritus, Bert Bank. I'm sad to say that in late June of 2009, Bert passed away at age ninety-four. But until a year or two ago, he always took his seat next to our statistician for each and every ball game, home and away.

Bert started the radio network back in 1953, a few years after he returned from serving in World War II, where incredibly, he survived the Bataan Death March. He was an amazing and inspiring person, who had the most incredible stories! (Like the one about playing golf with Coach Bryant or getting stopped by a state trooper with the coach in the car.) He was an inspiration to us all, and I will always appreciate his friendship and support, especially during my early days as the Voice of the Crimson Tide.

What a crew! (Back row L-R) Butch Owens, Tom Roberts, Tom Stipe, Ken Stabler, and me, (Front row L-R) David Crane (now the voice of the UAB Blazers), Brian Roberts, and Chris Stewart

FIFTEEN

Rammer Jammer

WHEN I BRAG ABOUT CRIMSON TIDE FANS, AND I DO THAT A LOT, I like to back up my boast with numbers.

My favorite line used to be, "What other college football team gets forty thousand fans at its spring practice game?"

Then Nick Saban came to town. Now I say, "What other college football team gets ninety-two thousand fans at its spring practice game?

Unbelievable.

In January 2007, Nick Saban was hired as Alabama's new head football coach. The moment the announcement was made, fans from Tuscaloosa down to Mobile up to Huntsville and back up to Birmingham couldn't shake the feeling that they had a serious winner on their hands. The thousands of fans who greeted him upon his arrival in Tuscaloosa and the tens of thousands who showed up for the Spring Game knew his reputation for molding a football team into champions. And that's exactly what Saban began to do.

Coach Saban operates much differently from the other six head football coaches I have worked with at the university. I emphasize that different isn't wrong. Different is just different.

Taping the coach's pre-game show with Gene Stallings.

In the past, I would meet with the head coach every Friday night prior to the football games. We would get together at the hotel or at the coach's home, and since I usually brought my wife and daughter along, they would visit with the coach's wife while he and I talked. We'd shoot the breeze, talk about our families, and then, of course, we'd talk some football. Later in the evening the coach and I would tape an interview for the Saturday pregame show.

Coach Saban prefers to do things differently. He and I meet on Saturdays, two hours prior to kick-off, to tape the coach's interview. In Tuscaloosa we meet in his office inside the locker room. On the road we meet in his office in the visiting team's locker room; or when the facility doesn't provide a private office for the visiting team's coach, we find another location. Our meeting place does not have to be fancy—at one venue we stood under the grandstands; at another we sat on a John Deere tractor in the grounds crew's equipment area. Our meeting place just has to be efficient. It must be close to the locker room (so the coach doesn't waste time coming and going) and private (so time isn't wasted with interruptions).

Coach Saban runs like a Swiss watch. He arrives for our meetings precisely two hours prior to kick-off. He is never early. He is never late. We sit down, I turn on the tape recorder, and we begin the interview. During every one of our interviews, I have always felt as though I had his complete and undivided attention. He gives me wonderful content. Usually, we are finished inside of ten to twelve minutes, at which time he says, "Got what you need?" I say, "Yes sir." And that's it. He then gets up and returns to his team to finish preparing for the game.

I have never seen a man so intense and so focused. Coach Saban has a clearly defined mission: to win football games. He adheres to a strict set of standards and has a proven method for accomplishing his goal. He proved his mettle as an incredibly successful college coach when he led LSU to the 2003 national championship. So I'm not going to complain if he doesn't like to make small talk. That's not what he's here for. The one and only thing he cares about is improving his football team and his program.

West Virginia native Nick Saban was born to be a college coach. That's what he loves. When he left to coach in the NFL for a few years, he missed the college game immensely. According to Saban, that's ultimately why he made the decision—which was not popular in Miami—to leave his position as Miami Dolphins head coach and take the Alabama job. Much was made in the national media of the fact that when he came to Alabama, Saban became the highest-paid college coach in the country. But remember, he was paid very well in Miami too. Wherever he went, he was never going to have to worry about where his next meal came from. But it wasn't just a dollars-and-cents thing with him. Saban loves working with college kids and teaching and molding them. That's a very different animal from coaching professionals who are paid to show up and do their job.

Before you can teach them, you have to get them here. And Saban is perhaps best known for his affinity for recruiting. His 2008 and 2009 recruiting classes, voted by many as the best in the country, included ESPN's top-ranked receiver prospect and Foley, Alabama, native Julio Jones. According to a 2008 *Forbes* magazine article, Jones's mother, Queen Marvin, said that when she met with Saban, he talked about education, which was a big plus in her eyes.

"Football won't always be there," she said.

In the same article, Saban revealed what he says to prospective players. "I tell them this is a forty-year decision, not a four year one."

It worked with Julio. He not only signed with Alabama; he distinguished himself throughout his freshman season, especially during the Tide's victory over Saban's former team, LSU, where he made seven catches for 128 yards. Jones finished his freshman year with an armful of honors, including 2008 AP SEC Freshman of the Year. On top of that, Julio was also elected to the U of A student senate.

Coach Saban sets a very serious tone and runs his football team like an ultraefficient business. The man at the top is responsible for all aspects of the football program, from recruiting and administration, to public relations. But more than anything, he is responsible for his players.

According to Saban, every experience is an opportunity to learn and grow. After the Crimson Tide's 41-30 win over the Georgia Bulldogs in 2008, the fans were thrilled. But during his postgame interview and again during our interview the following week, Coach Saban said over and over, "I'm happy." (In fact, he joked, "I may not look happy, but I'm happy.") "I'm proud of our players. But we did not do well in the second half. There were penalties and missed assignments. If it was a test, we passed. But we passed with a 75 instead of 95 or 100 percent."

During 2007, Saban's first year as Alabama head coach, the Tide finished the regular season 6-6, but an Independence Bowl victory over Colorado made the final tally 7-6, officially giving Alabama its second winning season in five years. Then, in 2008, Alabama went undefeated in the regular season, 12-0! Impressive!

No doubt the jewel in that perfect-season crown was the Iron Bowl win where Bama not only beat archrival Auburn during the season finale in Tuscaloosa, but shut them out, 36-0. It doesn't get any sweeter than that. But true to form, as soon as the cheers in the stadium were quieted and the hoots and hollers in the locker room tapered off, Saban was already focused and busy. Looking forward to the next game. The next lesson.

A few weeks into the 2008 season, it felt as though, once again, the world was spinning on its axis correctly! Alabama fans are often accused of being spoiled. But really, how can they not be a little spoiled? Throughout the rich history of the program—from Wallace Wade and the early Rose Bowls, to Frank Thomas and his multiple championships, to the unbelievable reign of Coach Bear Bryant—the Crimson nation expects and is used to success. That's the way it's always been and that's the way it will always be!

Being ranked number one—getting back to that point—was so rewarding for the players, fans, and coaches, and it certainly was a whole lot of fun for the radio crew. It was a fantastic year that also happened to bring some major changes in our broadcast team.

Following the departure of longtime color man Kenny "the Snake" Stabler, we tried something new. Rotating color men. Every week we welcomed a different guest analyst, all of them former Alabama greats, including Steadman Shealy, Jerry Duncan, Antonio Langham, Tyler

At the office, Bryant-Denny Stadium

Watts, Bob Baumhower, Prince Wimbley, Sam Shade, Fred Sington, Tony Johnson, Andrew Zow, Kermit Kendrick, and Chris Mohr.

Several of the guys had previous radio experience, but the old sage in the group was definitely Jerry Duncan, who became Alabama's very first sideline reporter in 1971. Coach Bryant, who was always dead set against a reporter working the sidelines, was eventually swayed when it was suggested that the role be filled by Jerry, one of his favorite players on his legendary mid-'60s teams. A few years after his playing days were done, Jerry Duncan grabbed a microphone and stayed on the job for twenty-four years!

It was a no-brainer deciding which game Jerry should do. He is a Tennessee-hater (a fact he used to make well-known on the air!), so we signed him up for the Third Saturday in October. As guest color analyst, Jerry enjoyed a great view of the 29-9 Alabama victory over Tennessee on the Vols' home turf. As a guest in the booth, Jerry finally got a chance to *see* a game. He used to say that sideline reporters are in the absolute worst position to see the field, a reality that our new sideline reporter, Barry ("Goal Line Stand") Krauss had been experiencing for himself. So we were especially glad that this year, ol' Jerry got his due.

Another guest analyst was Roger Shultz, the great center who anchored the offensive line for the Tide from 1987 to 1990. We had a lot to talk about with Roger, who had recently gained fame courtesy of the TV reality show *The Biggest Loser*. Roger, who partnered up with ex-Alabama lineman Trent Patterson on the series, lost some 55 percent of his body weight as all of America watched! He went from 363 pounds to 164 pounds in several weeks, losing what an NBC press release described as "the equivalent of a wide receiver from his mid-section."

Shultz wasn't voted the winner of *The Biggest Loser*, but his weight loss was remarkable, and his loss was our gain, or . . . something like that!

Before the start of each broadcast, whether our guest had radio experience or not, we reviewed the basics of what we do in the booth. I made sure to remind the guys that during the game, once I called the play, I needed them to talk. That sounds silly, but when you're not used to it, sometimes the tendency is to hold back. The analysts all were former players. They are the ones who have been there and done that, so I was counting on them to explain to the listeners how and why a certain play unfolded as it did.

The guys on the crew and I also reminded our guests that they were doing radio. On television the announcers basically put captions on pictures. The viewers can see for themselves a great deal of what is transpiring on the field. But on radio you have to paint the full picture.

One of our guests had never been on radio, but he did have some television experience, which, understandably, colored his approach. He simply couldn't help himself when early in the game he said, "As you can see," and "If you look right there . . ." I scribbled a note and passed it over to him—"Our listeners can't see!"—and to his credit, he corrected himself and did beautifully for the remainder of the broadcast. That was great concentration on his part. I do remember at the end of the game, though, when he took off his headset, looked over to me, and said, "Whew! That was quick!"

The guy was literally out of breath. I don't think he realized how much you have to say on a radio broadcast. You can't just say, "Coffee!" when Glen Coffee takes a hand-off. You have to describe every step of the hand-off—before, during, and after—to keep your listeners up to speed. It's not an easy thing to learn.

We had another awkward moment when I posed an on-air question to a different guest color analyst. I said, "That was a beautiful play, don't you think?" And the son of a gun nodded.

I immediately hit my cough switch, leaned over, and said, "Man, you can't nod on the radio!"

I take responsibility for that one. I shouldn't have phrased the question that way. From then on, it was only open-ended questions that don't offer the possibility of a simple yes or no answer.

The truth is, these guys did great. Every one of them appreciated the chance to sit in the best seat in the house. I've always said, one of the best things about my job is where I sit. Not only is there a fantastic view from the booth, but over the years an incredible parade of folks have stopped by the booth to say hello or to be interviewed during the broadcast. A highlight for me was meeting Mel Allen, the long-time Voice of the New York Yankees and the guy whom I used to fall asleep listening to on the radio when I was a kid.

Pre-Yankees, Allen, who grew up in Birmingham, was an early Voice of the Crimson Tide in the mid-1930s, while he was a student at the university. And since Allen went from Alabama to New York while I went from New York to Alabama, our paths had literally crossed long before we met.

Thinking back, I'm afraid I peppered Allen with a lot of questions about his New York days, all of which he answered graciously. I loved the story he told about having to do live commercials on TV. He said he didn't mind doing the commercials per se, but when he did the spots for Ballantine Beer, he'd have to pour the beer into the glass in such a way that it wouldn't fizz over. It had to have just the right amount of head on top of it. He would find himself in the sixth inning of a 2-2 game against the Tigers, worrying about not making a huge mess with a can of beer!

As every broadcaster knows, commercials are an important part of our job. Without sponsors, there is no broadcast. I don't think any of us really mind selling something now and again.

At Alabama, we have a dozen or so old-time sponsors who've been great to us over the years, including Golden Flake and Coca-Cola. ("Great pair, says the Bear.") But every season we get a few new sponsors. For instance, last year, Barry Krauss was our Cook's Pest Control sideline reporter. But over the years, perhaps our most unusual sponsor was Bovatec Coxy, a product that treats a condition in animals, primarily cows, called *coccidiosis*.

At one point, the company that manufactures Bovatec Coxy bought commercial time with Learfield Communications, which co-owns the Crimson Tide Sports Network. The advertising package, which was concentrated largely on agricultural networks, also included one live spot during each of our games.

So following a time-out in the third quarter, I would say, "Folks, if your herd is suffering from coccidiosis, and the udders on your cow are cracked and hardened, we have the solution for you. Try Bovatec Coxy . . ."

Then my color man, Kenny Stabler, would add commentary. "Now, let me get this straight," he deadpanned. "Do you swallow it or rub it on?"

We had way too much fun with that one. We were actually sorry the commercials only ran for a year.

Commercialization in sports is sometimes a controversial topic, and no one learned that lesson better than Coach Gene Stallings.

From 1990 to 1996, Gene Stallings steered the Crimson Tide, and in 1992, his understated, workmanlike team brought home the first post–Bear Bryant national championship. The coach was and is incredibly beloved in Alabama, not just for his winning ways but for his straightforward, Texas-style honesty and tough but ultimately kind approach.

One Thursday night we were at Baumhower's Wings Restaurant in Tuscaloosa doing the coach's call in-show. Previously that week, it had been announced that Nike was going to replace Russell Athletic Wear as the uniform supplier for the football team. This was somewhat controversial since Russell had been a longtime sponsor and was an Alabama-based company. But Nike offered a significant amount of money to secure the deal, money that the athletic department and the university as a whole could put to good use.

Anyway, for some reason, callers to the coach's show kept bringing up the Nike deal.

The first caller said, "Coach. Nice win last week. Loved that call on third and 11. But what I really wanted to talk about is that Nike deal . . ."

Coach Stallings answered the question very carefully and extensively and said, "Look, there was no choice. This had to be done. There was a responsibility to do what was best for the overall university."

Next caller. "Coach, congratulations on the win. I like seeing you throw to the tight end more. But I also wanted to voice my displeasure about this Nike deal. I think it's wrong . . ."

The coach gave a good, solid answer. Not as long as the first one, but good enough.

The third caller. "Coach, great win. Nice blocking on that punt return. But what about this Nike deal?"

You could see the coach stiffen up.

The caller continued. "What bothers me is that Alabama has never had to wear a logo on our jerseys, with the exception of maybe a bowl game. Alabama doesn't wear logos on our jerseys! We've got classy crimson-and-white jerseys, and I think it's terrible that we're going to have a Nike logo . . ."

Well, by now the coach had had enough. He didn't want to answer the question again. "Look," he said, "the bottom line is, for the amount of money we're being paid . . ." Then he started gesturing to the Nike logo on his shirt, but since we were on radio, only the folks in the restaurant could see him. "Look, for this amount of money, if we have to wear . . . this *swastika* on our jerseys, then we'll do it!"

Time to go to commercial. My engineer said into my ear, "Did he just say what I think he said?"

He did. So during the break I leaned over to Coach Stallings and said, "By the way, Coach, the Nike logo is called a *swoosh* . . . it's a *swoosh*."

In his grumbly voice he said, "What'd I say?"

I said, "What if I told you we had no Jewish listeners left?"

It dawned on him what he had said.

"Aw, heck!" he said. "They know I didn't mean nothing by that."

And like good radio people do, we just kept going.

There were no better times in the booth than the nine years that Kenny Stabler was at my side.

In 1998 I found out that the man known as "The Snake" would be joining the broadcast as our color analyst. I didn't know him. But of course I knew about him.

Stabler grew up in Foley, Alabama, and was a talented, all-around athlete. The New York Yankees (my New York Yankees!) offered him a fifty-thousand-dollar bonus to sign with them, but this Alabama boy grew up dreaming of playing for the Crimson Tide. So when Bear Bryant came to visit him and his parents, the deal was sealed and he was University of Alabama–bound.

He had big shoes to fill at the Capstone. As quarterback on the 1965, '66, and '67 teams, he was picking up where Pat Trammel and Joe Namath left off. As a sophomore, he played behind quarterback Steve Sloan, and the 1965 team won the national championship. The following year, despite not being named national champs, the team went 11-0 and became the stuff of legend. The Snake-led team famously defeated Nebraska in the Sugar Bowl at season's end, a team that outweighed them by about thirty pounds per man!

Snake's senior year of 1967 got off to a rocky start when he tore a cartilage in his knee during spring practice. He became frustrated when he couldn't practice and started skipping school and otherwise getting into mischief. Coach Bryant suspended him from the team, notifying him by telegram. (There was no text messaging back then.)

Snake fought his way back onto the team. He reclaimed his starting position and played brilliantly that season, which included his famous "Run in the Mud" during Alabama's sloshy, sloppy 7-3 victory over Auburn that year.

Post-Bama, Stabler was drafted by the Oakland Raiders. He meshed perfectly with John Madden's rebellious, love-to-hate-'em renegades, backing up Daryle Lamonica and George Blanda at quarterback his first couple of years. By 1973 he was the starter, and Snake-led teams visited the AFC championship game five times and beat Minnesota (32-14) in Super Bowl XI.

In 1979 Snake moved to Houston and played for Bum Phillips's Houston Oilers for two seasons. He capped off his NFL career with two years in New Orleans. After that, he took up the mic.

Initially, he worked for CBS, doing regional games with Greg Gumbel and James Brown. Then he spent several years working on the *Silver Bullet Stadium Show* for Turner Sports.

Then, in 1998, Kenny Stabler came home to Alabama and became the color analyst for the Crimson Tide Sports Network. From day one he was superb, and I'm quite sure I never saw him trembling during that first broadcast!

Kenny's presence, without question, made me a better broadcaster. No matter how much I prepare, there are certain elements I can never bring to a broadcast. I've never taken a snap under center in the SEC or the NFL. The guy wears a Super Bowl ring. Kenny can explain it, explain it clearly, and do it in ten to twelve seconds before we have to set up the next play. He's that good!

Mostly, Kenny is a natural, gifted broadcaster. His descriptions, and especially his phrasing, are completely unique. Where some analysts might slip into using well-worn sports clichés, Snake never did.

Once, during a lopsided game at Jordan-Hare Stadium, Alabama was beating Auburn badly. At one point the score was 31-7 and the stadium was completely silent, except for the maybe ten thousand or so Alabama fans. Many Auburn fans had left the game, and those who remained were totally subdued.

During one commercial break, Snake turned around in the booth and (off the air) said, "Man, it's so quiet in here you could hear a mouse peeing on a cotton ball."

He had us rolling. When describing a great defensive lineman he had played against in the NFL, Snake would say, "Yup. I've been under him!" After a hard hit he'd say, "That'll knock the taste out of your mouth!" or "That'll make you sleep on your own side of the bed!"

My daughter Elise (L) and wife Claudette (R) join me in Dallas' Dealey Plaza after visiting the JFK Assassination Museum that is housed on the 6th floor of the former Texas School Book Depository building in the background.

Once, Alabama was playing the University of Hawaii, which understandably had a lot of players on their team with Hawaiian and Samoan surnames. There was one player, Pisa Tinoisamoa, whose name was giving a lot of trouble to the Snake. He solved the problem, though. After calling him "Pizza" for the first quarter or so, he finally took to just calling him "Mr. T."

Alabama had a great linebacker named Saleem Rasheed, who later went on to play in the NFL. He was good, so his name came up a lot. Often, when Snake mentioned him, he'd call him something different. Abdul Salaam, Salam Aziz . . . it got to the point that even though he wasn't getting his name right, we all knew exactly who he was referring to.

When you travel with Snake, you learn quickly that you are traveling with a rock star. People recognize him right away from his Alabama days or his Oakland Raiders days. And basically, the minute they do, the decibel level goes up. It doesn't matter whether we're in Phoenix or Knoxville or New York City, people swarm him everywhere. I've never seen him turn down a request for an autograph or a picture. And he does it graciously. He genuinely seems to enjoy every person he meets, and whether we're on the Quad on the Alabama campus or a tiny rib joint in Fayetteville, Arkansas, or walking through the New Orleans airport, it always seems to me that Snake could stand there and shake hands and tell stories all day long.

Perhaps some of my favorite memories of our times together are the many times Joe Namath visited us in the broadcast booth. Joe always had (and has!) a standing invitation to come on the air, and every time this former Alabama star quarterback and recent graduate (Joe went back and finished getting his degree at the age of sixty-

Butch looks on as Joe Namath and I chat in the broadcast booth in Tuscaloosa.

four!) joined us in the booth, the chemistry between him and Kenny was magic.

I always say, I may be ugly, but I'm not stupid. If I have Kenny Stabler sitting to the right of me and Joe Willie Namath standing to my left, that's what Alabama football is all about. I'm smart enough to just call the play and shut up! Let those boys talk, analyze, and banter back and forth.

After the 2008 season, Kenny, of his own choosing, decided that he would not return to the Alabama broadcast booth. We'll all miss Kenny on the broadcast. But we also know that he won't be hard to find. Just look for a cluster of people crowding around a tall, smiling guy with a wild mane of white hair.

After the 12-2 season of 2008, Alabama fans have a lot to look forward to. Although the postseason was disappointing with the loss in the SEC championship to Florida and the loss in the Sugar Bowl to Utah, at the end of the regular season, Alabama was ranked as the number one team in the country. That's a title the Crimson Nation could get used to. Again.

Bryant-Denny Stadium in Tuscaloosa: If there's a nicer stadium around, I've never seen it!

Alabama's teams have won twelve national championships. We've been to more bowls than any other school in the history of college football. When you walk across campus on game day and see the miles of tailgaters and crimson-clad fans and bands and tents with banners, and then you walk into Bryant-Denny Stadium and every one of its 92,138 seats is filled, it's impossible not to be filled with excitement.

This is a no-brainer. Alabama is picking up where we left off.

Because Alabama is among the nation's elite, being the Voice of the Tide makes me the luckiest man behind the microphone. It's been a great, great ride. And Lord willing, it's nowhere near over.

I was the guest reader this day at an elementary school in Birmingham.

My dad, David, is the gentleman on the left.

I'm ready to climb aboard a Harley to shoot the opening segment for a TNN NASCAR telecast in Phoenix.

Only problem . . . I don't "do" motorcycles. On the air, it looked to all of America as though Ol' Eli was at home riding that bike. In reality, I had a good bit of help.

Claudette, Elise, Butch, and I enjoy time on the "Crimson Tide" in the waters off the coast of Ocean Isle Beach, North Carolina.

On a trip to Buffalo, Claudette and I had to ride the "Maid of the Mist," the boat that takes you in to Niagara Falls.

On a rainy day, Claudette and Elise meet the Buffalo Bills mascot at Ralph Wilson Stadium, the home of the Bills.

I've always loved Corvette Convertibles.

The loves of my life: My daughter Elise (who is now almost 20) and my wife Claudette who is now almost . . . oh . . . never mind!

Butch and Claudette holding the chairs down on the front deck of our summer home in Ocean Isle Beach, North Carolina.

About the Authors

BROADCASTER ELI GOLD IS BEST KNOWN AS THE VOICE OF THE University of Alabama's Crimson Tide, where he has provided the exciting play-by-play for twenty years. In addition to his Bama duties, this Brooklyn-born, longtime Birmingham resident also hosts *NASCAR Live*—a weekly, nationally syndicated radio call-in show. Gold is considered one of the most versatile broadcasters in sports, having done call-in programs and play-by-play for arena football, NFL, professional baseball, and NHL on radio and television. His many honors include four Alabama Sportscaster of the Year awards for his interviewing skills earned from the many talk shows that he has hosted, including the nationally syndicated *NASCAR Live* that still airs on over 400 radio stations through the Motor Racing Network.

M. B. ROBERTS IS THE AUTHOR OF FOURTEEN BOOKS. SHE HAS collaborated on several projects with Eli Gold, including *Crimson Nation* and *Bear's Boys: 36 Men Whose Lives Were Changed by Coach Paul Bryant*.

BRENTWOOD PUBLIC LIBRARY